# Ironman: Journey to Lake Placid

## James Armata 2010

# Copyright

# Dedication

*It is with the utmost of love, respect and gratitude that I honor my lovely wife Karen, and my adoring children Casey and Amy with the writing of this book. It is their continued support, guidance, and sacrifice that has been unconditionally provided over so many years that helped me to arrive at a place, I am happy to call my home.*

# Acknowledgements

Music has been inspirational and nostalgically pleasing, a way to re-connect with so many special moments! It is with great enthusiasm that I joyfully thank and acknowledge the many musicians and artists for providing such a driving force and tools for success.

www.asiphoto.com for the many beautiful images captured and illustrating those special moments!

A very special anonymous donor that afforded me the ability to maintain the integrity of my original works by covering some costs for licensing on music and photography.

The Dalton School with special thanks to Roy Samuelsen and the New Lab Technology Department for the many years of support as this wonderful community that is "committed to a tradition of life-long learning, and educational innovation" has helped me to reach so many goals and to "go forth unafraid!"

Bob Cook, Jose Lopez, Steve Tarpinian, Larry Parker, Barbara Cronnin- Stagnari, Rich Barkin, Bobby "Liebo to Liebo" Quinn and all my Long Island training and racing friends.

Aaron Schwartband for his inspirational story affectionately entitled "Aarons Song", Doug Fuller for his "Ode to Transition Bags" and the rest of the gang on the "Blue Page" for many years of love, support, training and racing advice.

My Bear Mountain buddies Tony Squire, Frank Moore, and Brian Carver, with whom I reached some amazing peaks!

Pete Cotter, Mark "Bernie the Attorney" Bernstein, and Rich O'Neill have been there from the start and inspire me to continue following my dreams.

My loving parents, Isabella and Tony Armata and all my family members including the Caratozzolos' that have allowed me to follow in their foot steps and helped to clear a more gentle path.

# Contents

## 2000 IRONMAN TRIATHLON AT LAKE PLACID:"A JOURNEY INTO THE SUN"

## 2002 IRONMAN TRIATHLON AT LAKE PLACID:"A JOURNEY BACK TO THE SUN"

## 2004 IRONMAN TRIATHLON AT LAKE PLACID:"THE LONG  JOURNEY BACK "

## 2010 IRONMAN TRIATHLON AT LAKE PLACID:"UNEDITED AND UNINTERUPTED"

# 2000 Ironman Triathlon at Lake Placid:
## "A Journey into the Sun"

# Introduction '00

"So you think you can stop me and spit in my eye, so you think you can love me and leave me to die, oh baby, can't do this to me baby, just got to get out, just got to get right out of here." There are no easy words or phrases to sum up an experience that reaches deep into your body and soul, testing your limits and leaving you dreaming about that moment when you come through clean on the other side. The song lyrics played on, the orchestra and symphony came together, the crowds were screaming and I was crying like a baby. My parents, strategically located at the entrance of the oval, with camera in hand, greeted me as I completed the 16 hour and 19 minute session with life, death and all it's mysteries.

I scanned the crowd desperately looking for my family. I came upon my sister, nephew and my precious daughter that was starry-eyed and comfortably dressed in her pajamas. I snatched her into my arms and headed for the finish line. The music played on, " and we'll keep on fighting 'til the end, 'cause we are the champions, we are the champions, of the world!" I broke through the tape and was reunited with my adoring wife and baby. The year long fiasco was truly a "Journey into the Sun", an educational experience that demanded efficient time management, proper planning, and sacrifice. More importantly, it was a year that would signify a reconfirmation in the belief that your faith, family, friends and health are truly the greatest gifts in life and you should treasure them always.

## Seacrest-Tobay/Point Look-Out

It was the summer of '99, which marked my first triathlon at age 36. I didn't know it at the time, but within one year I would have completed two triathlons, two marathons and an Ironman. I was originally motivated to become involved in triathlon training in an effort to improve and maintain fitness levels in a variety of ways. Too much of anything is bad for you. The combination of bicycling and swimming that would supplement my running was not only appealing, but also a smart way of training a variety of muscle groups while avoiding the pitfalls of over running. Unfortunately, this theory goes out the window when the international distance in my first two triathlons turns to Ironman distance within the year. I guess I knew that it would come to that given my desire to find the greatest challenge. I just didn't think that it would come so quick.

My friend Rich O'Neill signed up a bunch of us for this summer excursion in Oyster Bay. It's a triathlon rich in tradition and the numbers of participants continue to increase each year. The coordinators of the race run ten heats to keep it safe for all its athletes and they do a terrific job. This race will always be special to me because it was my first triathlon. It was also great to be in a race with Peter Cotter, my harmonica mentor, long time traveling buddy and a man that chased his dream. He is the Brew master and partner at the only Long Island brewing company in existence better known as Bluepoint Brewing Company. He had a vision and is fulfilling that landscape greater then any Van Gogh or Bobby Ross in modern times.

The significance of this race becomes even more magnificent when you examine the people that are conquering it with you. People that have the courage to follow their dreams and do it in a way that touches everyone in their path. I get together once a year with this group during the N.F.L. conference finals. The Farell brothers, Bernie the attorney, and most of the O'Neill family are just a few in attendence. We enjoy some hearty, robust brew from none other than the master himself and share stories of our year. We put entries into a journal for the upcoming year that includes a list of goals, phrases and of course, inspiring lyrics. We read what the previous journal entries included and indulge ourselves in the nostalgia that is our life. "Did you ever take that vacation, have another baby, build that deck, get that degree or finish that race?" It was wonderful to see the guys again this past year and follow up on our ritual. I arrived in the last quarter of the last game and shared some great stories of a summer gone wild. Conquering one of the greatest challenges of my life and finding out details of their success as well. And of course, entering new challenges. At next year's reunion, I'm hoping to tell the story of going ten times around Boston in the Chancellor 100 k!

And so, the details of the race are not nearly as important as the people you meet and those with which you become reunited. However, it's those first steps, the first experience that you reflect upon to help you in your future endeavors of racing. We would all like to improve our fitness and do better in each race. Therefore, hydration, nutrition, equipment and preparation are just a few examples of that which should be noted for the record and looked upon as a resource/learning tool for the future.

I went to Oyster Bay and Lido Beach the week before each of the races to practice on the course. These sessions proved to be valuable and would later be instrumental in my success at Lake Placid. I realized the value of such an experience and pulled some strings to make sure I went to "V&V" weekend in the mountains. This experience will be summarized in all its glory when the time comes.

Mental imagery is an extraordinary tool that allows the athlete to envision the course and better prepare for race day. The preparation for the swim course varies. In my first race, there was a slow start with many heats and sighting land and various other points to establish better orientation in a calm bay situation became the norm. In my second race it was a mass start, you nearly got strangled at the first buoy and the ocean waves were quite intimidating. In my third race (the ironman) the fog was dense, the cannon exploded and nothing could have prepared you for this mass of humanity that were swatting, kicking, and vying for position on the "sight line". A strategy must be prepared for each of the various waterfronts and an awareness of the type of start you will encounter becomes key to maintaining poise and focus for the race ahead.

The theme of mental imagery continues throughout the transition phase and onto the bike. Imagining yourself stripping down (easy everyone) and getting out of the transition quickly and efficiently can set the tone for the remainder of the day. The transition for the international distance becomes much more critical than that of an ironman, much like that of a 4 x 100 vs. a 4 x 400 in track. Each requires thoughtful preparation and imagery, while making certain you don't forget anything. Once on the bike, strong mental focus prior to race day helps you to establish pace, discover road hazards, anticipate gearing and plan hydration/nutrition while in motion.

I was "wet behind the ears" in my first two races and pre-race rituals saved me from much heartache and despair on race day. The simplest concepts of having enough air in the tires, a functional chain and a crank that would not fall off in the middle of the race were just some of my early lessons. The biggest lesson learned was to make sure that I had descent equipment going to the race. Equipment failure can break a day and destroy morale, especially when you've spent the entire year tuning up your engine. You must learn how to be a technician of your bike with basic repair skills and tools that can help fix the problem. All the training in the world will not help an ill-prepared bicyclist that falls to the mercy of road hazard and equipment failure. I realized that my Schwinn World Sport would not be sufficient for the challenge in the mountains that was still to come. I would need something special. I would need to find a trusty steed that I could love, care for and rely on to get me through 1000 miles of training and a 112 miles in the mountains on race day. It's not that different from relationships, but it's starting to sound somewhat ludicrous. The fact is, if your going to ride this baby for 6-8 hours in a competition and spend another 100 hours in training, she had better fit, be darn comfortable, reliable and willing to go the distance. Okay, so the bike does not have reasoning powers. The point is that you must be confident in the equipment you use and have the ability to make it work despite any failures along the way. I was aware that a purchase of this magnitude was well outside my budget. A descent bicycle that qualifies for such an important race would include a titanium frame, puncture proof tires, disc wheels, a comfortable seat, an odometer, a bento bag, aero-bars, and water bottles etc. I began pooling all my resources to help finance this magical vehicle, while exploring the many options that were available. I researched and questioned as many people that I could so that when I saved enough money from all my resources, I could make a smart purchase. More importantly, however, it was time to focus on tuning up the engine that would carry me through 140 miles of race and hundreds of miles of training leading up to that special day.

# N.Y.C. Marathon

I had been running marathons with the Achilles Track Club since '97. This is an organization that helps handicapped individuals pursue their dreams and continue athletic endeavors despite the difficulties and challenges that they must overcome each day. As noble as it sounds, I became involved with the club by virtue of some miscommunication that committed me for the race and just as quickly knocked me out. I found myself all pumped up, and nowhere to run. And so I turned to the club, volunteered for the marathon and have been running with them every year. The stories that come from this experience include wheelchair, blind, amputee and other various categories of courage, fortitude, and hope that brings a tear to my eye every time I envision these people crossing the finish line. This was truly a testimony of the human spirit soaring high in the sky and claiming victory at the conclusion of a spectacular day. Despite the wonder of it all, I hungered for more. I watched in amazement as these charismatic, courageous and strong willed beings pushed, pulled, and literally dragged themselves to the finish line in an effort to achieve their goals. It was time that I started doing the same. It was time that I stepped it up a notch and find a real challenge. I found it!

## Aqua Center at Eisenhower Park

It was the beginning of winter break around the middle of December. I'd been training to a moderate degree at this point, which followed my first two short distance triathlons over the summer and my annual fall marathon around the five boroughs. It was time to get serious. I drove my car on Hempstead turnpike toward the Aqua Center. This was a beautiful facility, one of the biggest in the Northern hemisphere and built for the 1998 International Goodwill Games.

I began questioning myself as I continued to drive. In a serious and concerned manner I thought, "What have I done?" "How am I ever going to complete 140 miles in one day?" The music on the car stereo began playing as a familiar, nostalgic and quite ironic tune stroked my ears. The introductory rhythms of the song "Ironman" surrounded me and put me at ease for a moment. Despite the irony of the song, I continued to doubt my reasoning for getting involved and seriously questioned my fate in this race. The words from the song came through in a triumphant manner and delivered the answer that I'd been looking for in this moment of insanity. "I am Santa Clause!" It was a parody. I realized that I should maintain a strong sense of humor and not take this challenge so serious.

The goals of the race are simple. Develop and maintain a discipline that will: a) encourage tremendous fitness levels, b) improve the skills necessary to be successful, c) associate with as many new and interesting people as possible and d) accomplish this in a manner that will be economically, socially and be reasonably feasible for a man with a full time job, two young children, wife, mortgage, etc. In actuality, none of these goals are simple, especially the last goal that pieces everything together, that which is my family. Fortunately, I have my Karen, an adoring and lovely wife of nine years that blessed me with two beautiful daughters named Casey and Amy. It was through their love and support that I was able to accomplish all these goals in a spectacular fashion. Any man or woman that has a family understands the sacrifice and planning that goes into such an excursion. I do not have all the answers for families that embark on such a challenging journey, but Jim Morrison summarizes it best by chanting, "I tell you this, no eternal reward will forgive us now for wasting the dawn!" Goals were now in place, but more importantly was the understanding that family must come first, maintain a sense of humor and let the music be your guide. I'd be a total hypocrite to say that I was completely successful throughout my training in keeping these goals in tact. There were numerous times when my family would suffer and take a back seat to my training. I was often much too serious and occasionally the lyrics turned cynical as I fell into lapses of hopelessness and despair. We often understand what the goals are and the rules that go along with accomplishing those goals, but are mere mortals and will stumble and fall on occasion. The trick is to get back up, reorganize and continue to work while considering all those around you.

Training sessions at the Aqua Center began with some light weight lifting, treadmill work and of course, swimming. I met a woman named Michele whose address was "runalot" and we immediately clicked. She told me that her goal was to complete an ironman in France. Michele was always at the center working hard on her swimming technique. She had floats for her feet, paddles for her hands and a waterproof pad complete with drills. She was obviously serious about what she was doing, but not too serious. Michele was instrumental in changing my poor swim technique. I never became motivated enough to break out the paddles or work on different swim technique. I was quickly convinced that my approach stroke developed over the years of lifeguard training was not going to work. I had to retrain my body to crawl efficiently through the water. I had to keep my head down and my legs up if I wanted to be successful after the 2.4-mile swim. I may be able to finish the swim, but my improper technique would have thrashed my legs, zapped my energy and left me wilted on the side of the road within the first loop of the mountain. It wasn't long before I was logging in miles and hours at the pool and feeling confident of my swimming ability. On one occasion however, I swam 2.5 miles and without any warning signs, cramped in the final lap. Both of my calves knotted like balloons and my confidence was shattered. I straddled the ropes, remained calm and tried to relax my body. The last thing I wanted to do was call for assistance. I managed to get myself to the side and emerged from the pool like a wounded animal. I realized that I may have pushed too hard and that it's important to gradually build up mileage. I also realized at this point the importance of hydration and nutrition, especially in the water in which a mistake could prove fatal. I approached each swim with a lot more respect and applied this knowledge later when I began open water swimming at Jones beach. I carefully hydrated before each session and made sure that I supplemented my diet with potassium that is supposed to relieve the body of severe cramping.

It was important that I gained a better perspective on exercise and diet at this juncture and to remember my lessons learned without consequence. I also came to the realization that I needed to do more research and work on a more systematic approach to training, diet and exercise. I needed to chart my progress and keep a careful watch on my program. A carefully charted program can help in numerous ways. It allows you to closely examine the work in each discipline, provide appropriate amounts of time in each discipline and also help to schedule rest days. An appropriately designed program will illustrate peeks and valleys of training and recovery, while avoiding injury from a careless program.

## Ironman USA Comment Page

A place you can call your home. A sanctuary filled with humanitarians, doctors, lawyers, teachers, students, mad scientists, gnomes, bikers, singers, virgins and veterans. The list is endless and the loving, caring, compassionate, life-beating pulse of the world resides in this place. I've alluded to the fact that the people I've met along the way on this journey are the most important aspect of this adventure.

I've mentioned some good friends and family that helped me get started and made sure I reached the light at the end of the tunnel. I would like to introduce a few more characters, and I use that term in a most affectionate way. Yakabo is the gentleman responsible for steering me in the direction of a systematic approach to my training. He sent me a program that allows you to chart the progress of all the disciplines and provides monthly summaries of your progress. The data is compiled on a calendar that runs from Monday to Sunday and then transferred to the "spec" sheet. The breakdown of weekly run, swim, bike and miscellaneous training helps to oversee your program and plan accordingly. The graphs help to illustrate your progress in a color- coded fashion that further helps you to identify strengths and weaknesses of your program. I enjoy the miscellaneous category because I can include yard work; snow removal and other household chores that must get done and still consider this as part of my training regiment. I always found it extremely motivating because I would be excited about building those towers each month to even greater heights. I would sometimes come to the realization that at the conclusion of a particular week I was lacking hours and would go an extra session or two on the weekend.

I was also excited about the versatility of the program and used it in my fitness classes at the high school to encourage extra credit. The students could choose any four disciplines and chart the hours using a personal calendar. This program became a professional tool that the students can use to help motivate themselves to greater fitness levels while making a conscious effort to explore many forms of fun and enjoyable activities. Roller blading, ice skating, dance, basketball, horseback riding, paint ball, hiking etc. were just a few examples of that which could be charted and illustrated using this program. I found a way to systematize my program and include the many disciplines of a triathlon and also make solid progress in my profession.

I continued to go back to the comment page for advice and support. I was confident that I was in the right place to get information and begin my bond with other folks that happily and joyfully gave of themselves. My spirit was dashed as a cynical comment page peep responded in a negative and immature way to one of my questions. He was quickly displaced by a courageous, considerate, new to the ironman page herself and better known as Kelly Kelly Kelly from St. Joseph. She shrieked over the page and in an instant exposed this intruder, warning him to bury his ugly, fowl-mouthed face in the sand. She reminded him that this was a place where people come to ask questions, find information and enjoy endless laughter from some nonsensical banter. Soon after, others followed and I found myself at home again. Hammy welcomed me aboard his Mardi-Gras float, while Laser-Jet- Hellion, Susan Marston Vickery prompted me to sing another Grateful Dead tune for the crowd. Oreo-Jo supplied endless rebuttals to Johno's political plight, while the Mad Professor continued his work in the laboratory pulling the wing off of flies. Doug Fuller was at his best and voted man of the page for his continuous flow of information and quick time response to any question. He would always make you feel welcome and just when you didn't think you could handle any more training; he would put you on a pedestal and make you feel like a king. "I'm just so amazed that Fleet (a.k.a. Armata) could clip in for the first time in his life and have the guts to register for this event."

The Garv, Art the lung, Goodtime (who rode today), Puskas and Shaq were an endless resource for bike information, while Dev, Barry the Kona express, coach Jean (and her sidekick Jamie) were inspirational in their conversations on nutrition as well as years of ironman experience. There was the Canadian Barhaven Express Club with Douglas, Schep. Winnie, Randy, Princess Catherine, Adrian, Heidi, all the Ricks and all the Mikes (MIEKS), all the kings horses and all the kings men, as well as the local Westchester club with IronDon, Caryn (my torch barring partner), and the warrior goddess. There was an eternity of resource and inspiration from Rotoman, Doc Rob, Stud Dan, Traci, Pancake boy, Lambrides, EJB, Sundance, Geoffrey, Naugs, Cliff, Pete, Dave, Candyman, Aaron and Alley Elvis. There was Kinger and Woodman, my rock and roll buddies and who could forget the Boston Boys, BBB (first on the page), Patrick and Terry. When you headed North to Vermont, there was Nannok and the very special Bruce that managed this journey while struggling with diabetes.

When you headed East to Long Island, there was Gary that struggled with back problems and of course my main man Andre that pushed me through our first century together on the service road of the L.I.E. And then there was R.B. that I would later learn struggled through the competition after a serious accident in the spring. He's better known as Burke and shares much of the same philosophy, ideologies and passions that are the driving force of our lives today. The web masters are Marc Roy and captain Kirk, of which without their efforts, none of this could have been possible. I'm painfully aware that someone has been inadvertently left out, but certainly not forgotten. I've tried to include as many names as possible to depict the incredible forum that exists and the wonderful people that have been there from the beginning. This section of my report is an effort to simply introduce the characters from the page. The story lines that follow will most certainly paint a more colorful picture and better illustrate the magnificence of the people that I've encountered.

# Jenny the Pinarello

It was close to spring break in the middle of March. My training was becoming more intense and I was primarily using Central Park as my stomping ground. One day a week would be slated as half ironman day. I would run two loops in the park early in the morning and finish with thirteen miles, ride ten loops after work that totaled 60 miles and then go to the pool and swim a mile and a half. These training days proved monumental in terms of conditioning as well as huge confidence and morale building days.

I met a gentleman named George that rode the park in a fixed gear and was an awesome bicyclist. We worked on cadence and gearing throughout our ride and pushed each other through some tough miles. The continuous debate about low gearing, high cadence vs. high gearing and a less consistent cadence were some of the issues I had to resolve during these sessions. Hammy, Fuller, Garv and Shaq were always instrumental in helping me sort out the virtues in both methods. High gearing can promote strength, especially on hills, while low gearing and good cadence is a must for this ultra distance race. I worked on both methods and found much success in my riding. George was obviously a proponent of cadence based on his training in a fixed gear. He helped me realize that ultimately one must be strong and consistent in riding, especially over great distances and that cadence is the key. I still see George from time to time, riding happily in the park.

Despite my newly acquired wisdom, I still lacked confidence in the park as little old ladies with straw baskets on the front of their 1920 bicycles were passing me on hills. I hooked up with my colleague's friend and he took me under his wing. Paul, whom I'd known for years was a master at cycling and brought me on some training runs. He taught about proper clothing that can help reduce drag and reminded me of the importance of hydration while in motion on the bicycle. Little things like correctly tipping the water bottle to avoid spilling precious fluids to bigger things like making sure you have spares, tools and some knowledge of bicycle repair to ensure a successful ride.

Paul introduced me to a friend that raced in the 90's with the Tour deFrance. Michele was known as a "rabbit" or "pusher" on the tour and had an arsenal of bikes. He was a kind, Rastafarian man that entrusted me with his baby. "Jenny" was the name given to this beautiful red Pinarello, with Campy components and authentic Pinarello signature. I promised Michele that Jenny would be treated well and that she would be taking an extraordinary trip to the mountains with me that summer. I spent numerous weeks laboring over my decision. I spoke to my comment page Gurus, salesman and consulted various other resources before making my purchase. Unfortunately, budget was a big concern, but I wanted to buy the best with that which was in my means. The brand new Cannonade, with basic components, but certainly more state of the art technology that included handle bar shifters and shinny new wheels was certainly tempting. It was way over my budget and so I went with the Mercedes Benz of bicycles in an older model. We settled on a price and in parting, Michele gave me his racing shoes and wished me luck on my journey.

I proceeded to the local bike shop to give Jenny a tune up and pick up some other necessities that my friend Paul mentioned. Adam was the technician that gave me the most help and actually helped save some money on the purchase price of the bike. I purchased new tires that matched the frame, bento bag, odometer, water cages, bottles, Co2 cartridges, bike pump and a new seat. Jenny was suited up and ready for action. I exited the shop and a gentleman shouted, "that bike is beautiful!" "What's her name?" I smiled and replied "Jenny."

# Spring Break

It was now the middle of March and I was on a two-week vacation. It was time to explore Long Island and what better way then to be riding on my new red Pinarello. I studied the map and decided to go to Jones beach and ride along ocean parkway until I reached Robert Moses. This loop could provide me with some terrific wind resistance along a road free from traffic with nothing but miles of pavement and a stiff ocean breeze.

I suited up in my wind resistant bike clothing, packed my water bottles with ice cold Gatorade and headed for the beach. Although the beach was only six miles away, I wanted to drive my car and avoid any problems on the road. When I arrived, I took the bike out of the car and clipped in for an exciting ride. It was only my second time clipping in and I was a little nervous. I practiced in the parking lot for a little while before heading out to the road. I decided that it was time and began my trip down the parkway.

I was a little frightened because I was in uncharted territory. I was literally learning how to ride my bicycle as well as attempting to navigate a course that was only confirmed by sighting on the map. All my fears and anxieties came to a screeching halt when I heard sirens whaling from behind me as a park ranger instructed me from his jeep to pull over. I was only a half-mile out and was still trying to clip in to the bicycle. Apparently there was a sign that forbid bike riding on the highway. I missed the sign as my eyes were focused on the pedals. Such was my lack of experience that I crashed shortly after being pulled over to the side of the road. I found myself trying to pedal in the sand and before you knew it, I was on my back and still clipped into the bike. The ranger instructed me to ride back to my car on the shoulder were I proceeded to crash again while trying to navigate on the soft, sand ridden shoulder. I didn't know it, but at the time I was pulling a "Giles". The ranger proceeded to write me a ticket despite my pleas of ignorance to the ordinance.

And so, on my first ride, I received a traffic ticket. I had my day in court and the D.A. apologized for such a ludicrous letter of the law type of ticket. I actually enjoyed telling my story in front of a packed courthouse as the tale of my ticket turned quickly to a heroic adventure of cycling gone wild en route to the ironman.

Determined to find a place of safe, unimpeded cycling, I drove to Eisenhower park, which was also my swimming arena. I began circling the two-mile loop only to realize that dodging children on tricycles, avoiding lame walkers that covered the entire path and sliding by numerous pedestrians going into the aqua center was not going to work.

On one occasion, I thought of the bright idea of going down by the pond to provide some nice scenery to my ride. As I glided down the hill toward the pond, there was a pack of Canadian geese flapping around along the path. I soon found out to my dismay that they were not moving. I tried to veer out of the way and was left with only two options. I could head first into the pond or head first into the pond. I went to a third option and dumped onto the concrete covered in geese poop. I thought we had a deal with the birds? Needless to say, this ended my days of cycling in the local park.

## Huntington/Massapequa Bike Clubs

I called some local bike clubs and found out about weekend rides. The meeting place was at the Fleet bank in Huntington. I thought this was rather ironic given the fact that this is my "handle" on the page and decided to join them for a ride. We had not even left the parking lot and suddenly a loud crash came from the middle of the crowd. I fell in front of the entire club that was preparing to "lock and load." Despite my flushed cheeks, and turtlehead, I moved out with the pack. We went through treacherous conditions that included steep winding roads, huge hills and sandy shoulders. We only went about 20 miles before stopping for bagels. Clearly, this was not benefiting my program goals. I needed to find some safe conditions with a solid pace and lots of mileage. Instead, I was getting a scenic tour of the North shore and experiencing a casual Sunday outing.

The following week I went to the Massapequa Bike club that met at the train station. It was at this club that I was introduced to a gentleman named Greg that did the ironman in Lake Placid and was the multi-sport coordinator, another fellow named Glen that raced for years and navigated the rides as well as my swimming partner Michele. It seemed to be coming together. I went with the second level cyclists, who would push the pace, take roads that were safe, and put in the mileage.

I returned each week and began going back-to-back days. On one occasion I went with the top bike division and was dropped within the first 10 miles. I was reunited with Glen, one of the old timers that could kick my backside even on his worst day. He worked with me on my cadence and helped me to navigate the service road of the expressway, which would later become my primary training ground on Long Island. I felt at ease with Glen and like so many others before him, he guided me through posture and technique that would pay big dividends come race day. He recommended that I adjust my aero-bars and position them in a way that would put me in a more upright position, thus taking pressure off my back and promoting more efficient cycling.

Each week I would take the tour with Glen's group whenever possible. He offered a safe ride, one that observed traffic signals and kept a close watch on the pack so that no one would get lost. Unfortunately, he was not always at the rides and I found myself subjected to packs of cyclists that didn't pay careful attention to traffic signals and would leave you in an instant if you fell behind. I found myself running lights and pushing the pace in an inconsistent manner as I tried desperately to stay with the group. I was in a position that left me out in the cold on too many rides. I couldn't go with the less experienced group because it lacked the serious miles and pace I needed. I couldn't work with the elite pack because they were too strong for me to keep up with on any given day.

On my last ride with the club, I was left at a light and had to navigate back to the train station. I decided that if my training was going to be solo, then I would decide the location, time, pace and distance. This decision alleviated a lot of stress in terms of time management, navigational problems and all the other difficulties with racing with the club. The benefits of the clubs included comradeship, pacing, motivation, skill assessment etc. I learned all that I could and it was time to move to solo training.

# Long Island Marathon '00

The training to this point was going well. I was doing most of my runs around central park in the early morning and averaging thirty-five miles a week. I was swimming twice a week and averaging three miles. I would bike two or three times a week for an average of one hundred miles and weight training was twice a week at night at Hewlett High School. The program was well balanced, but more emphasis needed to be placed on cycling and less on running.

I was building up mileage for the marathon and was excited because this was to be my first solo run since I began doing marathons in 1997. Prior to this race I'd been involved with the Achilles track club and helping others get to the finish line that had disabilities. And so, with the opportunity to run in my first race, I worked hard at improving my running and planned this race as a training run. I figured with all my supplemental training, this would certainly be a great time and one for the books. I still needed to remember that it was meant to be a training run and that the usual taper and recovery guidelines that are generally followed for a marathon was not to be followed in this race.

I continued to log on miles throughout race week and even biked fifty-two miles and did two hours of property work the day before the race. The morning of the race, temperatures soared to a high of 92 with Long Islands' infamous humidity factor. I was confident that I would do well, despite the heat that had appeared for the first time in the season. The situation was that prior to race day, there were no significant hot temperature training days. The result was over a dozen people hospitalized and hundreds of people treated for heat stroke/exhaustion, while countless others opted for the half-marathon. I would have none of that, paced well and enjoyed my training day. I took in fluids at every station and methodically plowed through the course. This was the first marathon that I wasn't pushing a wheelchair, sighting for a blind person or working with a courageous amputee victim. I was out there by myself, and loving every minute. Suddenly, I came upon a woman that was staggering and falling back on her heals. She was suffering from severe dehydration and was in trouble out there on the Wantagh Parkway. I helped her to what seemed to be the only shady tree in sight and was fortunate enough to get help from the paramedics that were only a mile down the road. The slight detour reminded me of the seriousness of the conditions and helped me to regain perspective on the goal of the day. It was a training run and yet another opportunity to help out a fellow athlete that got in a little over her head on a day that was brutal. I sang and rejoiced for the remainder of the race and continued on my path to the ironman, being thankful that I could repay someone, anyone for all the help that I'd received to this point.

## Veterans and Virgins Weekend

The weekend retreat in the mountains of Lake Placid was to be the sight where experienced tri-athletes would work in conjunction with the many novice individuals' that were hoping to complete their first ironman distance. It was an opportunity to put a face to the many comments, suggestions, advice and friendly banter that had been the forum on the comments page. It was also an opportunity to ride the course and become familiar with the terrain. I mentioned the importance of mental imagery and the role it can play on race day. This was to be one of the best decisions made during my year of training and always regarded as a special weekend. The weekend prior to this adventure was my first century ride. Andre Lapar, a young college student that lived in the area met me at the service road of the expressway and we finished our first century ride together. It was a great confidence builder and with that landmark of training, I headed for the mountains.

The rain started on Friday and reared its cold, ugly head throughout the weekend. My bike flopped in the wind on the rack of my car all the way to the mountains. It was another thing to learn and thankfully did not come with a price. Simply tying the tires with the straps was one of those little bits of information that could've alleviated the pressures of a trip that was already filled with so much uncertainty. There seems to be so many little details that need to be learned to be successful at this sport that one must learn to be patient and allow time to be the greatest teacher. I like to keep lists of information and reflect back on that data. There is far too much to remember, especially when everything is so new.

We arrived in Lake Placid and got settled at the apartment above the Gap that we rented for the weekend. Once settled, we drove to the camp ground were most of the people were staying. It was brutally cold this weekend and the tents soon came down and the cozy cabins were quickly filled. My daughters loved "oreoJo's" campsite most because it had pink flamingos and other assorted tropical island decorations. She didn't know it at the time, but her grounds were redecorated by some of the more creative, mischievous comment page "peeps".

It wasn't long before introductions were being made and folks that were chatting for months were meeting for the first time. The first people I met were in the campground headquarters. There was Garv with this huge, white, cowboy hat and standing next to him was Art the lung. We walked back to Jo's campsite and met Hammy, Fuller, Randy, Mike, Douglas and his family. Eventually we were introduced to BBB, Patrick, Terry Nannook, Bruce, Junior and Johno. It was a packed house and the training would begin early the next morning. We met at Desperados for dinner that evening. Casey was thrilled to meet Hammy, while Amy demonstrated the infamous "double-fist pump" to the roar of an excitable crowd, especially Patrick.

It was a brisk, damp morning and although I felt confident with my fitness level, I was uncertain about my ability to navigate and maintain pace on the mountain. Hammy made me feel comfortable and lent me a pair of shoe warmers that saved me on this ride that would prove to be blustery and challenging. Everyone was preparing to leave and I was thrilled to supply a clutch bicycle pump for a number of cyclists. We departed from the campground and began our ride into town. This part of the racecourse is the most challenging. It's the last ten miles of the course and it's up hill all the way to town. There is a huge section of steep hills depicted by the writing on the road as "Little Cherry," "Little mamma," "Little bear," and "Big mamma." I like to refer to those sections as "Little Jerry" and "Mamma tried, " 'cause I taught that weepin' willow how to cry, cry, cry."□

The sharp, sandy right turn at the top of the hill leads you to yet another smaller hill and to the smoothly paved roads that surround the lake. This is also the section were all your transition and special needs bags are placed on race day. You follow the lake and go to mainstreet at which time you come down the hill through the town, pass the grill and begin the first set of "hard ups" past the ski jumps. I made a mental note of the major sections that I believe to contain difficult and steep grades as well as the annoying and sometimes even more challenging endless row of "chain ring hills."

Once you get over that first hard section of steep grades you cycle on a number of chain ring hills and pass a section that is narrow and frightening, close to the rivers edge with traffic moving quickly on both sides. Suddenly, you find yourself on a three-mile slip and slide ride into Keene. This was the most frightening, exciting, "please don't crash and die" piece of highway that I've ever experienced. I held on for my life, slid carefully off my aero bars, said a prayer and then smiled. I reached the bottom of the hill and was thrilled to see the pack of cyclists waiting at the breakfast shop. My odometer charted 39 miles per hour down that ride from hell that makes Space Mountain at Disneyworld look more like the merry- go-round at kiddy land. I never would've gone that fast, but the entire time I was afraid of getting lost on the mountain and was playing catch up with the pack. I knew this was a huge hill, but wasn't quite prepared at the time. In the middle of the descent, I realized that this was the hill everyone was talking about and throttled down in an effort to simply stay alive. I remember that Garv had pleaded with anyone that lacked experience to get off the aero bars on those downhill until the skill has been acquired and confidence gained. I also remember Hammy teaching me to use my elbows to steer properly and safely, avoiding any unequal forces on the right or left that could flip you in a second. It was great to see the smiles on everyone faces, especially those people that never experienced such speed and velocity on any pervious ride.

It was time to continue to the second round of hard ups and into upper Jay. The course leveled off and the scenery was phenomenal. We blazed past rivers, sang songs and breathed in the air. I was pretty excited at this point, pumping away and enjoying the day. The veterans were reserving their energy. They knew that the last set of hard ups were yet to come. This section of highway separated the pack as we encountered the steepest section of the course that would lead us to Hazel(nut)ton road. Once again, I was concerned about loosing the pack and getting lost, but Patrick and Johno were always close by and this was helpful in moments of despair. A couple of guys doubled back to let us know about the turn at Hazleton road. I headed down the out and back and was pleased to see most of the gang coming from the other direction. I wanted to reunite with the crew and in a "Giles-like" fashion tried to make a quick turn and dumped on the side of the road. This was the last that I would see of anyone that day.

It was around this time that the rain started falling. It was getting cold, damp and dreary and I was feeling a little bit lost. I found my way back to the campground and proceeded to town. I was excited about finishing my first loop of the mountain, but demoralized by loosing everyone and uncertain about the possibility of finishing another loop. I continued on my path to the town and was starting to wonder if I was going in the correct direction. Eventually I saw the writing on the street and knew I was in the right place. I returned to town and stopped at High Peeks Cyclery in search of some other cyclists. It was pouring rain that felt more like sleet. I was shivering, wet and felt alone. I was determined to finish the century ride that I came to accomplish this weekend. I wanted to brave the storm and challenge myself to one more loop of the mountain. The "other Rick" was the only person still around and so I considered going with him on the second loop. I decided to pay the mountain a little more respect and figured that I would wake to ride another day. It was uncharted territory, the mountain was slick and dangerous, thus my day was done.

I completed sixty-six miles that day in some tough conditions. I made a great decision to call it a day and plan to ride again the next day. I found out later that Rick flatted and had a difficult time getting back to town as the rain turned into torrential downpours as mother nature dared anyone to cross her on this day upon that mountain. I changed out of my wet clothing and geared up for a run to the campground.

"Be on my side, I'll be on your side babe, together we can get away. This much madness seems so hard to handle, it's impossible to make it today. Down by the river." The song echoed in my heart as I enjoyed one of the best runs of my life from town to the campground. It was pouring rain and the river flowed in the same direction that I was running. It was down hill to the campsite and I had Mr. Blue Bird on my shoulder. It was truly a wonderful day of training and I find it amazing that you can experience so much peace and tranquility at the conclusion of any given day. The "runners high"/ "endorphin like feeling" reached new heights on this day as I truly felt a spiritual awakening. The landscape was magnificent as the mountains touched the sky and the river flowed endlessly. I arrived at the camp and was greeted by the Boston boys, Terry, Patrick, BBB and others. The guys offered me some warm, dry clothing and we laughed while telling stories of the day's adventures. I remember describing my day and illustrating my marvelous ten-mile run to camp. Terry was especially touched by my experience and simply responded, "Amen, brother Fleet." The excitement and aura would soon pass, as many of the guys were already packing up camp and heading home. Bruce, Nanook and Hammy were among some of the guys that had to depart early from our training weekend. It was sad to see them leave, but I knew that we would be reunited again on race week.

The following day I connected with Rick and Giles as they graciously gave me another tour of the mountain and helped me to log in another seventy miles on the bike. The weekend was concluded with a fifteen mile run on the course with a girl named Luina from Canada. She was third in her age group at ironman Canada and demonstrated excellent running technique as well as informing me about some helpful nutritional information. She recommended "Metrx" bars that have a granola type texture as opposed to the traditional power bars that I did not care for in my training. We discussed the importance of hydration and before you knew it we had gone the entire first loop of the run course. The weekend summary included one hundred thirty-six bike miles, twenty-five running and a world of inspiration and confidence as I continued my Journey into the sun.

## Ten Weeks Remain Prior to the Dance

It was becoming quite clear that race day would soon arrive and the remaining weeks of training would be critical for the outcome of the race. I continued logging miles on the bike and was comfortable on all my long runs. I was working methodically on "bricks" in different combinations. Some days I would swim and cycle, other days cycle and run or swim and run. The swim would always be first because I respected the water and didn't want to take any unnecessary chances of "bonking" while in the water.

I was doing all my swimming at Jones Beach and getting used to my wet suit. Despite the fact that lifeguards were present, I was always cautious in my approach. Perhaps too cautious and although I logged in a great number of miles, my swim training lacked intensity. The fact is however, as long as I was training in the water by myself, I was going to be extremely careful and be assured a safe return to the beach. Perhaps the lesson learned is to get involved with a masters program and find swim partners for the open water training.

This advice plays an even bigger role in my training based on the fact that with only six weeks remaining I ripped my Achilles on a day gone sour. It was one of those days when you get out the door late, sit in traffic, break your bicycle pump and go to a different plan of action. You try to make up lost time by increasing the intensity of your workout. Include in this description being totally frustrated by the original plan getting lost and the result from the carelessness becomes quite costly. I went to Dr. Rozbruch, a friend from the Dalton community and whose opinion a value and trust. He told me that I should not run until the day of the race if I expected to see the finish line. He told me that I also should not "clip-in" on the bike. He suggested raising the heel to alleviate the pressure on my calf, which at this point was also injured. This could be accomplished with orthopedics and also by wearing cowboy boots. I thought that Garv, the gentleman that wears a cowboy hat and ironically lives in Dalton, might be conspiring with Dr. Rozbruch in an effort to create a western theme among all triathletes.

I dismissed this theory and found all sorts of other paranoid delusions to focus my attention. The level of uncertainty just reached an all time high. I would be permitted to cycle, but not clip-in? I would be permitted to run, but only in a pool? This was by no means paranoia or state of delusion; this was a reality check smashing me directly in the face. I decided to compromise and planned my training according to a new, conservative and productive method that would hopefully net positive results.

I stopped running completely and developed an aqua jogging program at my darling mother in laws house. I was able to train and have a terrific visit at grandmas a couple of times per week. A situation that appeared to be drastic turned into something very special, as the children and I saw more of grandma in those weeks then ever before and I was able to regain my confidence.

I started swimming three times a week at the beach and was also getting out on the bike between one hundred and one hundred- fifty miles a week. I was not willing to compromise with clipping-in on the bike, but rather made an adjustment in the cleat that moved my foot up further and alleviated pressure on the Achilles and calf muscles. I sometimes put on cowboy boots, but not in a medicinal way like the doctor suggested, but because I, much like Art the lung, also wanted to beat Garv.

I'm hoping you can understand the humor in this last statement about my Texan friend, Garv. The point is that without a sense of humor and an ability to overcome obstacles that appear to be dead ends, you cannot succeed in life. The ability to overcome diversity, put a positive spin on what appears to be an impossible barrier may prove to be the greatest lesson learned. When my aero bars snapped two weeks before the race, I laughed. Mostly because it was either laughing or crying and I thought the latter of the two would be best. It was yet another blessing and not a disaster as it would have appeared. The bars were reinforced and the situation, that might have happened on race day, was prevented by occurring prior to the big day. Find that positive perspective, follow that gleam in your eye and walk with a song on your heart all the days of your life.

# Race Week

It was three a.m. and I didn't need an alarm clock to alert me to the fact that it was time to head to the mountains. It was nostalgically pleasing to travel at this time because this was the way in which my parents traveled to the mountains. I carried my girls from their beds and tucked them gently into the car. The excitement in our children's eyes was priceless. I knew that wonderful feeling of having a chill in the air as my imagination soared to a place that I'd never been before, one that I would never forget.

We arrived in Lake Placid and the town was packed as the annual summer outdoor games were being sponsored that week. We settled in at the condominium overlooking the boathouse and marveled at the view of the mountains. The next day I took my final ride around the mountain and became reacquainted with the landscape, making final notes of the different sections that would challenge me in the following week.

I continued a mild taper program that week that only consisted of swimming, some light jogging and some tune-up rides on the bike. Each day I swam what I believed to be the distance for the course. I began to get discouraged at my time and started to worry about the two hour and twenty minute time limit for the swim portion of the race. I was getting around the lake in an hour and that was too close for comfort.

Tensions continued to mount as all my aches; pains and injuries were now surfacing. I began concerning myself with my equipment and started to lose confidence in the repairs made to my bike, more specifically, the aero-bars. My wife and family could do no more to help and were on the verge of packing up and going home. They had endured my training for an entire year, but were having great difficulty dealing with my radical behavior as we closed in on race day. Things were starting to come apart at the seams and it became apparent that I needed to fall back on some basic philosophy that carried me through previously diversified, seemingly impossible conditions.

I decided to read the letter Hammy sent to me and reflected on his words: "Remember the great training you've had and have powerful confidence in it all week long. It's payoff is around the corner, in a day long blur of dreams come true, emotions at all reaches of your personality, the realization of the power of fulfillment and accomplishment and in the beauty you will see of yourself as if you were watching yourself plow, sear and gracefully glide easily through the water, across the roadways and over the pavement which your feet never touch. And no matter how long it takes you, take each moment as an entire, discrete moment connected to endless, countless others and remember the blur of the day as a vivid step in your life."

This reflection was just the beginning of what seemed to me to be indicative of Michael the arc angel with all his angels and saints triumphantly marching into my life to help save the day. The events that would follow in rhythmic succession made me feel as if Bob Marley himself whispered in my ear "don't worry, about a ting, cause every little ting is gonna' be alright." I stepped out on the balcony to greet some friends that I knew as a child. The Zamoyta's are friends of my parents that have a house in Saranac Lake and wanted to come for a visit. When they arrived, I noticed some people in their back seat and assumed it was their daughter and children. To my astonishment, it was Isabella and Tony, my parents that drove from Florida to support me on the day of the race. This was indeed a wonderful moment and truly inspired me beyond my wildest dreams. I just want to make my parents proud of my accomplishments. They raised six children and instilled in all of us love, faith and hope. They were the sign I was searching for that week and presented itself at the time I needed it the most.

The following day my sister Sue arrived with my nephew Michael and gave great support to my wife Karen, which allowed me to go and concentrate on the details of the race. I attended some clinics in the village that focused on confidence and some race day tips. On Friday there was a gathering at the beach with all the folks from the comment page. We shared stories, exchanged some imported brews (for post race consumption) and discussed last minute details for the race. I had the opportunity to provide the music for the evening with some solo acoustic songs on harmonica. This gathering was short lived as the local law enforcement pleasantly and tactfully broke up this illegal gathering. They allowed us to continue our social gathering for about an hour and then asked us to kindly disperse and wished us good luck in our race.

It was now the day before the race and all the final details needed to be completed. Transition bags filled, Bikes racked in the oval, pre race massage by Dr. Rob and let the ceremonies begin. We lined up in the church parking lot for the parade. I was asked to carry the torch along with Caryn from Rye N.Y. It was quite the honor and my daughter Casey proudly held my hand as we marched through the village. The crowds were cheering and I thought this was spectacular that I was given the opportunity to lead the parade. We reached the oval and were introduced to the crowd as the inaugural Ironman winners! "Please join us in welcoming Thomas Hellriegel of Germany and Heather Fuhr" Although we were excited about the introduction, we quickly corrected the man and he reintroduced us as Caryn and Fleet. We then proceeded to the torch lighting area where Caryn graciously allowed me to do the honors. I climbed up the ladder and prayed the mechanical torch would not blow up in my face. The excitement of the day passed. We had our pre race-dinner and I reviewed the list for the next day to be certain all the fine points were covered. St. Agnes church had a beautiful ceremony and the priest said a special blessing for all the athletes. The stage was now well prepared and it was just a matter of putting it all together on race day.

# The Cannon has Sounded

I awoke at 4 a.m. as if it were Christmas morning. I couldn't wait to open my presents or in this case receive the gift of a successful race that I'd worked all year to accomplish. Breakfast was outstanding and I remember being in the best of spirits as I spoke in a German accent and felt the power of Arnold Schwarzenegger within me. I was ready for the task and as always had a terrific supporting cast. My lovely wife Karen, who supported me all this time made sure I ate well and got me out the door like a mother of a child on their first day of school.

My sister Sue drove me to the oval along the back roads because I still had to place my special needs bags in the appropriate locations. She was a great help leading up to race day and her support will never be forgotten. We gathered at the water and the fog was thick as pea soup. The helicopters were circling over our heads and the only question that remained was wheather or not the fog was thicker then the tension that filled the air. Suddenly and magically came a voice of comfort and joy. No, I didn't see the lord, that comes later, but certainly a messenger of the lord. Susan Marston Vickery emerged from the fog and with a comforting smile wished me good luck and told me that I would Rock! It was great to see a familiar face and receive such encouraging words, but nothing could've prepared me for the beginning of this race. The "Star-Spangled Banner" played over the intercom and "Who let the dogs out" echoed in my ears from the first day that I arrived on the pier in which that was playing.

The cannon exploded, you could hear the roar of the crowd and fifteen hundred people began thrashing and kicking their way along the sight line. Imagine bobbing up and down with no place to go. You swim forward and get kicked in the face or slow down for a second and someone nearly pulls you under the water. I took a moment to calm myself and then made a break for the inside of the sight line. I was afraid I would be disqualified for being inside the ropes, but they were allowing it given the density of the fog. I watched in amazement as some people swam for the boat at the conclusion of the first length of the race. I guess they had enough and decided this wasn't for them. Soon after, the crowd thinned out and I was able to get into a rhythm and focus on my stroke. It was thrilling to finish the first mile and a half because based on my time, there was no way I would miss the cut off for the transition to the bike. I came out of the water in one hour and thirty- six minutes and the expression of joy on my wife's face, and the sigh of relief knowing I made the cut-off was a terrific way to start the day. My dad was smiling from ear to ear and I know he was proud at that moment and thinking "this is awesome!"

I took it slower then most through the transition because the sensation of getting out of the lake was strange. I needed to get oriented to the land again and it was as if I just came out of a washing machine. I meticulously geared up for the Bike course and was greeted by Mr. Doug (I have an answer to all your questions) Fuller. He was a volunteer and I could think of no greater way to go through the transition then with Doug guiding my way.

I headed to the start and another volunteer complimented me on my Rock & Roll Salsa Jersey. This was the type of support we all received throughout the day and it's amazing how many wonderful people there were on the course that helped you successfully complete this race. The first loop of the mountain was smooth and I listened to the advice that Dev had given to me on one occasion. He reminded me to save some legs for the second loop and to be careful about going out too strong.

I finished one lap of the mountain in 4 hours and knew that I would have to do better on the second lap or risk missing the cut off time. I paced, hydrated and ate throughout the entire first lap. The second lap went well, but I started to feel alone out there on the mountain. It was helpful to see Patrick on the course and he appeared to be pacing in a similar way. The only difference is that he stopped to fix flats, while I spent too much time filling my camelback and setting the course record for urinating. I learned that using bottles supplied on the course is a much more efficient way of re-fueling, rather then re- supplying the camelback four times during the race. The rest was positive and may have proved to be a blessing as I began experiencing unusual heart palpitations as I neared the ninety-mile mark of the course. I believe that this may be attributed to the use of Afrin, a nasal spray that helped clear my passages and allow me to breath. The pollen count was brutal that summer and I suffered worse then any other time in my life. I learned that this product was affecting my breathing patterns and was frightened at this point in the race. I decided to slow my pace and listen to my body, making sure that breathing was restored and that my condition would improve.

It just so happened that around this time I was making my turn onto the three- mile uphill when I spotted a familiar face on the side of the road. It was Patrick and he apparently flatted again. Only this time he was not fixing his bike and appeared to be mumbling under his breath. I think he was saying, "I've got to beat that little gnome named Johno, but I'm out of spares!" The technician that pulled over offered some assistance, but did not have a spare tube. I reached into my bag and gave Patrick my spare and prompted him to get himself in gear if he expects to make the cut-off time. Patrick has expressed his gratitude on several occasions and has declared me as someone who saved the day. I maintain that the "Savee" became the "Savior" as that final rest stop was the miracle I needed to help restore my heart rate and prepare me to reach the 5:30 p.m. cut-off back in Lake Placid.

I reached the top of the hill and started calculating my pace and the time that remained. I realized that I would need to average 20 M.P.H. for the remainder of the course if I was to reach the finish line with a comfortable margin. I became frightened because I knew that on my best day I couldn't possibly average that speed in the final uphill battle back to town. I began pushing the pace all the way down and back on Hazleton road, taking full advantage of any declines while working extremely hard to keep a strong rhythm on the bigger sections of the course.

The goal was to get the pace above 25 m.p.h. to allow for the section of the course in which the slower pacing hills could have be packing my bags before getting a chance to fly on the marathon course. I waited all day to get off my bike and get to some familiar territory and nothing was going to get in my way. I pushed all negative thoughts from my mind and continued to blaze through the course. I passed the campgrounds and was all too familiar with that which remained in my path. A flat on this section of the course could be detrimental to my finishing time. Once again, I pushed those negative vibes from my being and throttled forward.

I reached the section of the course at the bottom of the hill that begins the final steep climbs of this course. There was a woman on the side of the road just sobbing and appeared to have lost her will to continue in the race. I reminded her that this was the last set of hills and that the finish to the bike course was only two miles away. I told her again, only this time said that she looked fantastic, finished 110 miles of this beast and that we are almost home. I told her that she had thirty minutes to go two miles on her bike and that she could rest after she gets to the next transition. She smiled, got off the ground, onto her bike and raced to the finish like a true champion. I arrived at the oval at 5:10

p.m., made the cut-off and knew at that moment that although there was still a marathon course to navigate, I was already home.

My wife, children, sister and nephew were all at the transition to cheer for me and give me that final push to the marathon course. My wife, Karen, remembers that I looked terrific coming off the bike and was also confident at this point that nothing could stop us from crossing the finish line. She recalls how gingerly I handed my bike to the volunteer as if to say "Thank you Jenny for getting me here, I didn't expect to have no fear, I didn't want to cause no fuss, but thank you for being my magic bus!"

There were others that would arrive at the transition zone and as the volunteers promised them a safe return of their bicycle, the response was one of total alienation. One cyclist said, " I'm done, now you can keep it!" Perhaps some were less fortunate from the technical aspect and spent the day fixing flats, changing cables and sliding chains back on the bicycle. I considered myself fortunate throughout the day and was thrilled to be able to help some of the less fortunate folks that came across my path that experienced technical and psychological breakdowns on the road to the ironman.

## These Boots Were Made for Walkin'

The plan was to go out to the run course and try to get in before the sun went down. This would require a four-hour marathon and at the time seemed realistic. Suddenly, reality set in as every ache and pain that I'd experienced leading up to the race surfaced at mile three on the downhill section leading out of town. I felt my calf, my hamstring and my ankle all pull at once as if too say, " we're done for the day!"

I began to feel dizzy and disoriented as the rest of my system tried joining in like a choir on its encore presentation before it was intermission. I wasn't calling it quits and slowly and methodically raised the curtain for the final act. I shortened my stride and began humming a familiar tune by Bill Withers known as, "Ain't no sunshine." The melody put a smile on my face and my body relaxed. My body started to become familiar with that which I've done so well in my past, to run and keep running. I thought of "Forest Gump" and chuckled some more.

I started to see friends like Rotoman and Oreo Jo who were trying to beat Rick Baird. I was happy, relaxed and among friends. Unfortunately, many of my friends were a lap ahead of me and they did not appear as jovial as myself. I didn't let that discourage me; continued methods of positive talk and let the music be my guide. I arrived at the twelve-mile mark of the course and experienced a total breakdown. It was 8:00 p.m. and the people on the course were encouraging me with all the wrong words. They would repeatedly say, "You're almost there, it's just another mile or so, and you just have to get to the end of this road!" They did not realize, and perhaps people should be more aware, that I had another three hour and thirteen miles to go before calling it a day.

I wanted so badly at that point to run to my family, be held ever so tight and tell me that's it's okay that I didn't finish! It was getting cold, dark and I just wanted to go home. Suddenly, from out of the darkness appeared a bright light and his name was Andre. My century brother and training partner was there in my most needed hour and with that visit came inspiration, hope and joy once again. He said to me " Do it for your century brother and don't forget all those Long Islanders that you represent!"

He reminded me that my family is waiting for me at the finish line and with that pushed me back out onto the course. I began my second loop, filled with energy and desire. I saw Douglas from Ottawa and he was like a wounded animal at the side of the road. He told me that he was going to walk the rest of the course and that he was having difficulty urinating and also could not take in any food or liquids. He encouraged me to move on and so I continued plowing along making certain to re-hydrate at every station. Based on the information that Doug gave me, I realized that I was in pretty good shape. I was still taking in plenty of fluids and was also able to rid myself of any wastes without any difficulties. I was concerned about Douglas but knew that he was a veteran ironman and could take care of himself. He eventually finished before the cut off point at midnight, but not before his wife and children sent him back on the second loop.

Our wives and family deserve so much credit for the hard years of training that goes into such a race. We are all in it together and nobody is willing to experience the dreaded "DNF"(did not finish), especially our families that put up with so much all year long. This was a lesson that I was not willing to learn and not one that our families should have to live with or ever have to experience.

It was getting dark and lonely on the course. The only light came from the occasional glow sticks on the runners left in the field and the lighting that came from the water stations. It was certainly a good time for reflection as the moon and the stars become your only guiding light. I began to reflect on the many people in my life that have been so important over the years. Dave, Mike and Michele that I grew up with and whose children now come to my humble abode and play.

My musically inclined, brother extraordinaire' named John, whose compelling lyrics speak of the pain from losing a sibling in a tragic car crash at an early age transcended through his music the message of salvation: "Days can be crazy, nights can be so cold, it makes ya' wonder why you're here" begins to ring more passionately then ever before on the cold mountainside. My warm-hearted brother Tony, Lynn, Anthony and my baby sister Theresa that I miss so much from Florida comes to my mind as I make a pact to go visit next year.

The names and the faces keep coming to me as I continue on what is more commonly known as the "death march shuffle." It's as if I need to thank all the people in my life just in case I don't make it to the Olympic oval back in town. My extended family at the Dalton school flashes through my mind as the voices from the Physical Education Department, the Faculty Review Committee, the Parent Teacher Association, the children I coach and friends like "Scholl" and "Quain" extend their voices from the far reaches of their summer vacations, wishing for me a good night. The Dalton school is my home and their financial and emotional support on this venture in professional development is yet another indicator of the value I place in family and the fortune, which is my life on the upper east side of Manhattan.

I said my peace and it was now time to go home. My family and friends were patiently waiting in town to call it a night. The only hope they had was from the words of some of the finishers that knew me and consoled my wife, as the hour was growing dim. There was less than an hour remaining and the midnight cut- off was quickly approaching. "After midnight, we were gonna' let it all hang out, after midnight, we were gonna' dance and jump and shout!" The drama that existed rested primarily in the crowds of people that waited in the bandstands with baited breath as loved ones came into the light in that final stretch of road that crossed the tape. These are the real heroes of the day. Those mammas and pappas, spouses and brethren, cousins and volunteers that only wish the best for you as you go out and play on the mountain for an entire day. And upon your return, you're welcomed with tearful, joyful loving arms as your children whisper in your ears, "Daddy, you're my Ironman!"

# 2002 Ironman Triathlon at Lake Placid:
## "A Journey Back to the Sun"

## Introduction '02

"My love is alive and so it begins, foolishly laying our hearts on the table and stumblin' in. " Music continues to be a powerful instrument of expression as the lyrics and melodies set the stage and establishes the plot for this adventurous sequel.

The plan was to return to a place in which I learned so much about the challenges in life and attempt to answer the many questions that were left unanswered in the first act of this dramatic play. I would play the part of the preverbal guinea pig and with any luck; stumble safely across the finish line. The experiment, however, cannot be considered a success simply based on the outcome of completing the project, but rather in the careful dissection of the process.

The keys to success will be based on my ability to abstract information on training technique, nutrition and fitness and the application of these results in the race as well as in field of physical education and athletics. Furthermore, and perhaps most importantly, is that the process is an enjoyable one in which optimism and positive attitudes prevail in the most adverse conditions. Secondly, throughout the process, better methods of time management are established to help prioritize those things, which are most important in life that includes family, profession and friends. This explorative journal will piece together training, local events, ride reports, race revues and culminate with excerpts of the finest quality that defines the true meaning of the human spirit as well as reflection on and comparisons to the principles of education ... "don't you ever ask them why, if they told you, you would cry, so just look at them and sigh, and know they love you."

## Sugar and Spice

"When the dog bites, when the bee stings, when I'm feeling sad, I simply remember my favorite things and then I don't feel, so bad"

It becomes increasingly important throughout the training year that strategies of nutrition are used in combination with an assortment of positive and inspirational images. The body and the mind must be preserved and well nourished to enable one to continue moving forward. The point at which you find yourself being dragged is a signal that requires immediate attention. Perhaps it's food or water that the body demands to maintain pace or maybe it's the implementation of some positive mental imagery to help relieve stress and put that smile back on your face?

Maria makes it look so easy as she skips, dances and sings across the plains and we witness the hills coming alive before our very eyes with the sound of music. Perhaps, Ferline Maria does indeed have the answer? Keep it simple and it can be as easy as A, B, C, 1, 2, 3 OR DO, RE, MI. It is, however, important that some investigative research be explored prior to oversimplifying or establishing your plans. I found myself being overwhelmed by the amount of data and the ability to apply this information.

Hydration, protein consumption, absorption, digestion and excretion just to name a few concepts needed to be understood and applied. There was no simple answer, but rather a more complicated and tedious undertaking that would continue throughout the year. Much patience, experimentation, success and failure would be my experience as I prepared to find a simple plan that could be applied to a daunting task.

Fortunately, the second task of creating positive mental imagery to help forward progress throughout the year came a little easier. The combination of my built-in jukebox and countless blessings in my life including my family, friends and previous experience puts me safely on the mountain as the hills come alive.

## In the City: Knickerbocker 60k

"Up town, West side Manhattan, neon lights, all night long, I've got me a place to hide just six stops from mid-town, it don't matter how small, just a closet, you can call your home, in the city "

The weather report for Saturday was intermittent rain, 60 and clearing. 77 runners began the race in a downpour. I was dressed in a plastic bag that went from my neck to my ankles. I thought it was fitting to begin my first ultra in a downpour given my first marathon in '97 it stormed with 10 miles to go. I guess the difference is that there was only 10 miles, not 37. Anyhow, I smiled, pushed negative thoughts aside and began my race. I felt terrific after a couple of loops with the exception of my throbbing quad and soaking wet body.

I decided to save myself and pulled back on my pace, especially on the hills. After 3 loops and 14 miles the rain slowed and I made a good decision to change into dry clothing. The tricky part was changing my sneakers while balancing on a cinder block that was holding up the tent. My quads were swollen, but I managed to powder my feet and get socks and sneakers on without touching wet ground. Although dry and feeling fine, I was discouraged because of my condition and slow pace after only 3 loops. I reminded myself that running for 2 -3 hours in the rain, slightly fatigued already from flu-like conditions and just not doing well in the cold was a pretty good reason for my performance to this point. I pushed all negative thoughts out of my mind and continued.

The rain had stopped and I began enjoying the intimate company of the runners that is so heart-warming with this elite club of runners. The old timers humbled you to no end, but were a great source of inspiration, not to mention the handicapped guy that could barely walk! My marathon split was so discouraging (@5 hrs), but someone reminded me that it's not a marathon and you should not be at marathon pace at 26 miles. Despite some disappointment with time I chugged on, knowing it was all bonus miles from there. My wife and kids made it to the city and were a bright light with only 3 loops to go. Although I felt guilty about making them wait, knowing I had another 2-3 hours, I was thrilled to get hugs, kisses, and cheers at the conclusion of each of those loops.

I banged out the last loop in @ 45 minutes, grunting, groaning and pushing hard. I was going to finish strong and at least get in under 8 hours. I neared the finish and my daughters ran at my side across the finish line in 7:52:26. In conclusion, what interests me most is the nutritional aspect of this race. I drank @ 648 oz. of Gatorade on the course. Total fluid intake on day including coffee, water, juice and coke was 756-oz. fluid. I consumed 6 little Advil's, 4-shortbread cookies 1 multi vitamin and a cantaloupe in a fruit tree.

# Spring Fling

Saturday's pre-race ritual included 8 backbreaking hours in the yard. I was hosting a huge post-race marathon party at my humble abode and the edging, hedging, whacking, and mowing was being done for the first time this spring. I enjoyed every minute of this glorious day and it helped relieve pre- marathon stress.

My back was quite tight and so I began IB profaning it at intervals starting at dinner, bedtime and at breakfast. My darling Amy kept us up most of the night and I was pretty whipped the next morning. I took my vitamin, juice, cereal with raisins & bananas, slim fast and was out the door. My girls told me they will miss me and there was much love upon my departure to the start line. I realized the race was about to begin when the wheelchair guys stormed down the road. I jogged to the start a half-mile and the horn sounded.

My best start ever, right in front of the 5000 runners in this race. 4500 are only doing the half and so I'm in a pack of speedsters and went with the flow. I found my line and it was smooth all the way out. I felt tired, but great to be alive. We ran past the deli and I yelled to the owner standing outside his store to make that 4ft. Hero an 8 footer cause I'm gonna' be darn hungry when I get home. I got the feel of a real at home race and continued on, maintaining under an 8-minute mile. It was truly a remarkable day for running and I was not to be denied a PR. Many tunes popped in my head and I shared them with the crowd.

One water station was cranking Ozzy and Ironman was jammin' which pumped me up. I gave it right back to the h.s.

guys that had the box. When reaching the split for half & full I did some Morrison chanting, "This is the best part of the trip, the best part, I really like, what did he say?" and further pumped up the crowd and runners around me, while singing a Queen tune entitled "I'm in love with my car." I was cruising and feeling fine, but shortly after felt my calf pull hard and got back to the business of the race, reminding myself to not get so cute. Speaking of cute, when the gals at the next water stop asked if they could splash me, I had to use a little discipline to simply smile and thank them for the offer, politely grasping the cups and drinking as I did at every water stop. Many gallons of water in my system and I proudly can say; only 2 pee stops needed during race. Quite efficient stops I might add because the trees and bushes are readily available on this course.

I watched my pace and reminded myself not to kick too early. I reached the park and was greeted by the East Meadow Hs track team. I asked them to push me to my best mile time as I was trying desperately to get in under 3:40. Despite my best efforts in this closing mile, my body was slowly shutting down and reminding me that it has had enough. With each sprint attempt, the calves on both legs would yank at me and hobble me. I finally got a grip on it and paced in with a gal from Patchogue finishing with a 3:42:26. I shaved 10 minutes off last years time, finished 107/523 and 22/63 in age group. The top 5/10 overall winners were in my age group. My adoring family proudly greeted as always at the finish and post race activities were on. I suffered w/ a migraine the remainder of the day from too much fun in the sun, but hosted a quiet bash. Many of the neighborhood guests couldn't come to join in the "festivus" with the rest of us, which worked out good considering my condition. This was some difficult recovery for me and yet another major step in the direction of respecting so many of my page peeps that toe the line and turn in performances that are outstanding, and truly an inspiration to the human race. Peace, love and joy to you and yours.

## Bear Mountain

I was up most of the evening awaiting the challenge of Bear Mountain. Uncharted territory, city limits, bridge excursions, traffic, trucks, wrist- wrenching downhill, quad-busting uphills, a crash, a flat, HHH (hot, hazy, humid and of course Heather) or was that Stephanie? Either way, it was enough to make a grown man cry! Three Litespeeds, One Serrota and well, ya know, Jenny the Pinarello. Stephanie was a top local triathlete, Tony, a Hawaii/Florida Ironman finisher, Head of Mt. Sinai Surgical and Dalton parent, Eric a two-time Lake Placid finisher and Anthony, a tough son of mid-ship gunner.

Departure was at 6:15 a.m. from 87th and park, up Riverside drive and across the George Washington Bridge. Some tough 90- degree angles to maneuver and a difficult U-shaped sucker that almost crushed me before starting. I lost the pack as they stopped at the first town for coffee and so I started a lone trip up 9w after refueling at the local deli. The gang showed up and I questioned where I was and what I was doing. It was truly a beast and one of the most stressful rides ever encountered. I could not go aero based on ignorance of road conditions, downhill and uphill terrain. I held on for my life the entire way, which added three fold to the difficulty level. It didn't kill me, so I guess I'm stronger, but beginning to question this as a lifestyle that's really not for me! Despite my negative thoughts fueled by one rider that constantly reminded me that the next few miles would be brutal, nasty, impossible, but salvaged by Tonys' optimistic approach and funny antics as well as safe guidance, things went relatively well. "So that's what a hill looks like?" It never ended! It was a continuous gauntlet of hills. If you weren't getting crushed going up you were holding on for your life going down. "Satisfaction, satisfaction, keep me satisfied, I've got the love of a hoochie-coochie woman, she's calling from inside, she's calling from inside, try to get to you..."

The two "miler" and then the five "miler" almost broke me, as I had to do everything in my power out of the saddle just to keep from tipping over. Finally to the top and the suffering had just begun. A gorgeous thirty- second view and then back down the mountain. My wrists hurt from holding on to the breaks on the way down. I thought that going south to the bridge meant downhill all the way home. I could not have been more wrong! Once we got to the bottom of the first big hill it was time to climb up some monstrous section without having any fluidity from a lack of spinning on the way down. I was out of drinks and the mountain was just smashing me in the face! I lost the crew and just muddled through the town of Haverstraw, which is a nightmare of huge Mack trucks bearing down on you without mercy. Finally refueled, found the crew and continued on the course.

In my usual slow form, I was once again shot out the back and struggling to stay with the pack. Suddenly, one hundred yards ahead and I see Anthony clip Eric's wheel and down he goes for the count. I raced to the site and we quickly got him out of harms way. He had bloody knees and tender wrist with minimal bike damage. Shortly there after, we were on our way and I was relieved that I was not sucking on anyone's wheel or the damage may have been much worse. I basically wanted to ride solo and maximize training while simulating race conditions that does not allow drafting. It was a good decision and once again confirms my belief in the inherit dangers of riding club style. It's only a matter of time before someone crashes. Next up was a flat and I become the in house expert thanks to Garv and Fullers "roll your palms" method that put us back on the road in minutes.

I rode across the George Washington Bridge, some road rage with Tony on Riverside as he was, "Taking the Greyhound on the Hudson River line and in a New York state of mind," and then the suggestion to run in the park. Tony trashed me on every hill all the way up the mountain and climbed like an angel, but now I've got him right where I want him. It's my backyard and as I head for the loop, he bails and heads for the bridal path. I take my victory lap around the park and finish in pretty solid form.

One hundred and two of the nastiest miles ever ridden, smooth brick around the park in @6:30/50, which I'm satisfied with and just thrilled to get home. Tony makes a return trip the following week as I opt to go the flat Long Island course to smooth things over and wind up setting my own personal best on a century ride at 5:30. I join Tony the following week to establish three consecutive centuries rides and thank the mighty Bear for the hard lessons that will pave my way on race day.

## Sugar Mountain

"Well I've got those running blues, running away, back to LP, got to find a dock in the bay, maybe find it back in LP?" The plan was to invite a star-studded, 22 year old to stay with us in LP and distract my girls so that I could focus on my race. It worked like a charm as my good buddy ANDRE LAPAR makes an appearance, distracts my three angels (KAREN, CASEY & AMY), carries my special needs bag on race morning and also volunteers to carry the wheel chair racer from beach to water when in transition. A spectacular start to a day that had "Another season and yet another reason, for making whoopee."

I knew that no records would be broke on this day and the goal was to finish and enjoy as much of the day as possible, while helping as many people along the way. The first deed was at the "porta-pottie" in the oval as they were shutting down and telling all to get to the lake. The gal behind me was about to bust and so I moved her up in line and later returned her cap that she dropped. Found my way to the lake and upon entering saw many of our peeps including BBB (*Richard), JOANNE, KATE, ART, CHRIS, & AARON. I wished all a good day and settled for a hug from Aaron cause SMV wasn't there to send me off this time. The Cannon exploded and I waited one minute for the traffic to spill out and then hugged the line all the way around. Finished in 1:28, which was 8 minutes better from 2000.

I couldn't see out of left eye and eased into transition tent. 10 minutes in transition and off and riding with vision restored. I was feeling good to be out there and begin hydration and feed fest. I'm about 20 minutes better starting on the bike. No blowing up on the first loop and manage to eat all my bars and consume 2.5 gallons of fluid.

Andre is at needs station and sets me up with a sandwich and frozen drinks. He tells me the girls are napping, but they were in their little raincoats around the bend. I double back to give kisses and begin second loop. 56miles and really happy to be out there and ready to turn it up a notch. I arrive in Keene and at 42 mph in hailstorm, I spot a man down and slap on the breaks to make sure I make it through this section alive. Guys are floating in the left lane; "me and Jenny" are dropping like a rock. I get to the bottom of hill safely and the hail stops, the sun comes out and now it's summer time again.

SKYLER and the ALBERTSON FAMILY greet me with a smile a fancy sign that reads, "GO COACH ARMATA!"

I arrive at the 3-mile climb and remember how late in the day it was 2 years ago with PATRICK on the side of rode with his 3rd flat. This was a huge lift, knowing how far ahead I was from the previous year and I spun like a champ to Hazleton road.

One guy said that I make it look easy and I mentioned what FULLER told me about climbing with the weight off the bars. Others were complimenting Jenny and were thrilled about a true road bike on the course. I know JOE BONNES would've been proud and I wish I knew who he was at the beach when we spoke prior to the race (a 30 time Ironman Finisher/down-tube shift classic Pinarello Rider), but a magical moment all the same. Anyhow, at Hazelnut road, I saw my buddies, RON & AMANDA from DALTON and after the out and back we had a chat and I headed home. Big Bear and Little Mamma had nothing on me as I saved plenty for my run on those final climbs.

I was out of transition in 10 minutes and now an hour ahead of my previous time. A 5-hour marathon is attainable and the dream goal of 2 hours less is in reach. Go out strong, but the heat is brutal! Can't keep the pace and must begin shuffle that includes sponge, hydration, and pee stops every mile. "Porta-potties" were limited and the risk of disqualification for peeing outdoors was risky! Managed to hit some potties and other discreet locations. I arrived back in town and the goal slips away at the out and back as I change socks, sneakers and begin the 2nd loop with dry feet. Too much time spent, but now it's get in by 10pm. I was having way too much fun as I continued to sing, dance, smile and focus on finishing strong. I must finish without IV's or a medical tent visit and get home to the family in good health. And so, when I started spinning out of control on Riverside Rd., I cut off the engines and starting chatting. I told the BRITS they can't drink and proceeded to give up Advil to one guy and Tums to BIG FELLA. I only used 3 Advil's to this point and was only planning a couple more. SCOOT would be proud that I cut back and nearly finished without a drop. My man

GARV popped by on his bike and asked how Jenny treated me, FULLER, YAKABO & JOHNO were 'ironmanning' the Garv-aid station and I knew that the RICK'S, WICKED WANDA, RANDY, SCHEP, & our darling princess KATHERINE were also out there pushing us to finish. The last turn-around and "Two of us sending postcards, writing letters, on our way back home, we're on our way home, we're on our way home, we're going home. " I couldn't see the road under me, but I must try to run all the way to the finish and break an hour off my old time. Heading down by the lake I spot BURKE, he waits for me and we do a steady hard pace from the final turn all the way to the oval. He offers to let me go first in true "BURKETTE" form, but I've got some precious cargo to pick up. My darling KAREN hands me my double-fist pumping 3 year old (AMY) and my "Casey-Macey", splash and dash finisher and we run through the chute at 10:18pm, banging an hour off old time. No meds, no tent, just hugs, kisses and a successful Journey Back to the Sun.

The mighty BEAR JAMIE and COACH JEAN stayed with me on the mountain that day and I'll bet helped a few others like EILEEN that was caught in the wicked thunderstorm. They sent an angel named MAYOR WOODMAN to rescue her from the storms wrath as the entire town shut down and no one was to be found. Graham FRASIER has a heart of gold as he took a great risk to allow competitors to continue in the thunderstorm and cares 1000% about, and only about his people in this race. KIRK our Webmaster creates a place "Where everybody knows your name and they're always glad you came." Princess KATHERINE shows true iron spirit coming to this race and continues to amaze us all with her positive and optimistic attitude. My torch-bearing friend CARYN has it all together as she signs up again after disappointment 2 yrs in a row and is mirrored by her daughter LINDSAY that offers to bust her piggy bank to pay. HELGA and MIKE are on their way to Hawaii, DEV a ten-time finisher, GOODTIME & MARCY swim together and represent a truly great partnership. CHRIS, JEPPHY, UNKA, & BRUCE continue to inspire. BIG FELLA will get 'em next time. LABERGARATER, TRACI, GEOFFE? TOAD, NAJ, NG, WY, >G wilakas, oh great ghost, who else? KINGER, ANDY,

And to ALL OUR FRIENDS at home that cheered from your cyberspaces, ROTOMAN, KELLY, HHH, MAD PROF, DOC ROB, MIEK, CINDI, BANGER, ALI, ADRIAN, DOUGLAS, NANOOK, BARRYKONA, PUSKAS, NAUGARITAS, and HAMMY, I know you were there for so many of those miles.

## Aarons' Song

*Red (White & Blue) Storm Rising*

*Fans Cheer Through Thunder & Lightning*

*(Written by Aaron Schwartzbard)*

*After a busy day, I arrived at the finish line area just before 9:30 PM to stake my claim to a spot on the bleachers. I've never been one for a crowd mentality, or for hooting and hollering wildly, so for each finisher approaching the finish line, I was content to offer polite applause while the people around me screamed and danced on their seats. The seat I had taken was on the left side of the finish chute, about 20 meters from the finish line in one direction, and 40 meters in the other direction from the Lumberton, displaying larger than life-sized, real-time video of the athletes as they crossed the finish line. The music blaring from the concert sound system gave the scene a party atmosphere, and the volunteers who danced in the finish chute, throwing free gifts (emblazoned with the logos of the event sponsors) to spectators who screamed the loudest occasionally brought the crowd to near-hysteria. All the while, I was content to suck on my water bottle, and offer my best golf-clap, as if to say to each finisher, "Jolly good show, mate!'' at 11:00PM, 16 hours into the race, I started to see the flashes of lightning in the distant sky. Well,perhaps not so distant. Only 10 minutes later, I started to feel the first drops of rain. More drops followed them. And more, and more. Over the next 20 minutes, what started, as a light sprinkle became a shower, which turned into a storm, which became a veritable deluge? Race time was 16:30, and the race announcer announced that due to the electrical storm, everyone was going to have to get off of the bleachers. Further, they had to turn off all non-essential equipment. Off went the JumboTron, off went the music. The announcers had no more microphones, and the fifty-foot tall Blue Diamond Almonds Can balloon slowly became flaccid, before finally falling completely on its side. This was no longer a party. It was cold and wet, I was tired, and almost everyone else was fleeing to higher grounds (i.e., their apartments or rental houses). As I was starting to follow the crowd away from the finish line, I thought, "The only time I ever*

*choose to be out in this kind of weather is when I'm on my bike."
Of course, as soon as I thought that, I realized that I couldn't
leave. As tired and cold and wet as I was, several times in recent
memory, I've felt even MORE tired and cold and wet. And this
time, all I needed to do was stand around in the inch or two of
water that had accumulated on the ground, and offer
encouragement to folks who had been working hard for the last
sixteen hours --- folks who were about to reach a finish line that
they had dreamed of for months or even years. I took another
look at the finish chute. Most people had left, but there were still
enough spectators to line that final hundred meters one row deep.
So I took my spot and settled in for the last half-hour of a long
day. The volunteers and race officials, who had been dancing in
the finish chute, tossing free gifts to the audience had all left ---
all except for one. She was perhaps 16 years old, and she looked
like as much of a drowned rat as the rest of us. But she stuck
around, getting the crowd to cheer, working to keep our
enthusiasm up in the increasingly long periods between finishers.
That was no easy task now that there were several minutes
between each finisher and no music blasting out of the speakers.
In that time when we were waiting for the next finisher, we would
become quiet. Waiting. The people who were standing near the
last turn would see an athlete first. They would start banging on
the barricades that lined the finish chute. With that, the noise
would spread, until everyone down the line was yelling and
cheering. Even I found myself yelling louder and louder - trying
to give each athlete the homecoming he or she deserved after so
long on the field - with each passing finisher. As midnight grew
closer, the scene grew more spectacular. Mind you, this is not
how it's supposed to go. The crowds are supposed to build, and
the music is supposed to get louder. On this night, the only thing
that was increasing was the intensity of the storm. That, and our
enthusiasm. Though diminished in numbers, those of us who
remained to cheer for the final finishers were there because we
really, really wanted to be there. There was nothing artificial
about it, and in a way, that made it very special. With about ten
minutes to go, 16:50 on the race clock, a couple guys who
seemed to be school mates of the lone volunteer who was still*

*dancing around the finish chute jumped into the finish chute to help keep the crowd going. Now, not knowing if this finisher could be the last finisher of the day, we were giving each finisher a hero's welcome. I couldn't have screamed any louder. With 16:55 on the race clock, a race official leaned out from under the shelter of the grandstand, and held up a single finger to tell us that there was one more person on the course. ONE MORE PERSON! When the spectators lining the last turn started to bang on the barricades that lined the chute, the crowd erupted. We cheered and screamed and yelled and whistled and clapped and did everything we could to get this guy to the finish line. After he crossed the line, and we had settled down a bit, a race official leaned out from the grandstand once again with a single finger extended. There's ONE MORE PERSON out there! In the last five minutes, that happened about five times. And each time, we cheered as if our lives depended on it. Finally, someone finished at 16:59:13. The race official leaned out to tell us that there was one more person on the course. One more person? After so many hours, after 140.6 miles, after rain, then sun, then biblical storms, could this last person persevere for so long, and miss the 17-hour cutoff? But before any of our tired, excited minds could think about it too much, he appeared. He made it. He crossed the line in 16:59:37. Everyone took a moment to look at the grandstand, half expecting that someone would lean out once again, but relieved that no one did. Ah, mission accomplished. Everyone made it home safe. Just as we started to step away from the finish chute, looking for the least muddy path home, the folks at the far end, by that last turn, started to bang on the barricades once again. ONE MORE PERSON! I jumped back to my spot, glanced at the race clock --- 16:59:50 --- then started to cheer louder than I had all evening. As she came around that last turn, everyone had already figured out what she was about to learn: there was no way she was going to make it down that final strait-away before the clock rolled over to 17:00:00. She was going to miss it by a couple seconds. That didn't matter to anyone watching. We knew what she had done. She had stuck with this race through a long and difficult day. At this point, in these conditions, it didn't matter what the clock said, or what the race officials might say. What mattered was that she had made it here, and just as much as anyone else, who crossed that finish line this day, she deserved the title Ironman. But as she rounded that corner, and reached a point where she could see the clock --- 16:59:55 --- it seemed that her smile faded, and her posture dropped. It seemed for a moment that she might come to a complete stop as she watched the clock roll over. "It doesn't matter," I wanted to tell her, "you've made it, you're an Ironman." She kept moving forward, finishing as the clock read 17:00:13. The next morning, I picked up a result booklet. I didn't think for a moment about my own splits, or the times of any of my friends who had raced. The one concern I had at that moment, as I held my breath, turning to the last page, was whether the race director was wise enough to realize that anyone who made it through that storm deserved to be counted as an official finisher. I scanned to the end of the page, and to my great relief, I found this: Theresa Jordan, 17:00:13 Ironman!*

# Epilogue

"Well this will be the last time, this will be the last time, maybe the last time, I don't know?

The experiment on the surface appears to have been successful. Finishing time improved, smoother transitions, and greater friendships established, improved knowledge of fitness and nutrition.

And yet, there is so much more to be learned. I'm still curious about so many things. It's sometimes so difficult to take a chance in fear of taking a fall. "Carry on, love is coming, love is coming to us all."

The music continues to play and despite some levels of uncertainty, I'm sure about a few things. We must be willing to take risks in an effort to continue to grow. It's quite possible that we may fail or fall short of our goals, but should be commended for at least trying.

Perhaps that's the moment in time in which we reassess our goals and strategies and establish a different approach. It dawns on me that once again the process becomes the focal point. Derive exponential degrees of enjoyment in the activity, the people in which we engage with throughout our lives and spend more quality time with your children.

Respect yourself and others to allow excellence to be achieved and as the sun sets at the end of the summer, my daughter reminds me of what's most important saying, "Dad, you'll always be my best friend"...and kisses me goodnight.

# 2004 Ironman Triathlon at Lake Placid:
## "The Long Journey Back"

## Introduction '04

"Well the, danger on the rocks is surely passed, still I remain tied to the mast, could it be that I have found my home at last, home at last." The long journey back was entitled with quite the pun intended! This trip to the Ironman was an attempt to battle against an injury that plagued me for more than a year. It was an attempt to pump my fist in the face of the drunk that crashed into my car at a traffic light one evening and wreak havoc on my world!

I was one week out from running my 5th consecutive New York City marathon with Achilles track club, but fate would be serving up a new cup of pain. It seemed I would be the one needing assistance running anywhere at this point and the road back would be a long and arduous one. I count my blessings, however, for on that evening my daughter chose to ride home with her mom and escaped a tragic ending in the back seat of my car.

This section combines original letters from friends, the musical backdrop for impending movie ;-), and excerpts from my return to racing one year after the accident. I spent one year going to various chiropractors, physical therapists and finally decided to go with a holistic approach and get back to what I love most "Smiling and waving and looking so fine, don't think I knew you were in this song; And it was cold and it rained and I felt like an actor, and the thought of Ma and I wanted to get back there, your face, your race, the way that you talk, I kiss you, you're beautiful I want you to walk!!!"

# Post NYC Marathon

# 19099 FROM: Fleet Subject: gutted this one out Sunday, November 2, 2003 04:41 PM IP: 63.80.167.195 P-diddy ran about half of the race next to me and had an army of guys around him. I lost my colleague, Leslie Green, early in the race as she skipped across the bridge on her way to a very exciting first marathon finish. I remember back in '97 how excited I was in my first n.y.c. marathon, but I wasn't skipping, I was pushing a wheel chair with Achilles Track club.

Most painful race of my life! Cramping calf at 16 never let go. Tempted to bail, but that's never an option. Gonna' try and drive home and hope there's no traffic...congrats Aaron, it was hot out there today.

# 19100 FROM: Fleet Subject: home Sunday, November 2, 2003 07:42 PM IP: 68.194.95.207 Never been so scared in my life. Traffic was heavy, my heart rate was whacked and I prayed all the way home to make it back to my family. I can't figure out what happened out there today. I'm not sure if I over hydrated on the course, took too long of a taper (no choice based on being major banged up) or just wiped out from long soccer season, birthday parties, P.E. classes. I know that not sleeping all week is a huge contributor to my pain. Wife on anti-biotics w/strep, Casey w/virus that just ran its course and Amy w/double ear infection upon return from doctor. I must have something brewing to have been that week. "Anywho", can't complain given first long distance race since accident last October and some tough circumstances leading up to race. I made some promises on the way home tonight and amongst them include a serious look at this summer's ironman and my preparation w/diet, training and the many variables that must be looked at to get home safe.

## Hydration Issues: A Letter to Bob

In all my boring commentary about my weekend slugfest, I'm most curious about coming to some conclusions about hydration, water weight, racing etc...Salt tablets...my understanding is that they help retain fluids to avoid losing precious electrolytes and nutritional needs. They slow down the urinating and sweating process. Many of you use them, especially in hot weather conditions...Based on my 13 pounds of additional weight after the race and the fact that I consumed over 600 ounces of fluid, I'm wondering if a) I drink too much ( ez Patrick) b) my system already functions as if I was using salt tablets (although I do pee constantly) c) what are the symptoms and term used for over hydrating? Keep in mind...My pee is clear (a sure sign of being hydrated), I'm able to pee (A sure sign that all systems are still working), my recovery is relatively quick after a race (A sure sign that my methods are good)...and yet, still not sure of any of this :confused

Fleet, after reading your post I had a problem at IMLP 2003 with over hydrating. I had gained around 10 lbs during the race. They weighed me in the med tent and then gave me 4 IV's. The Dr. took blood and my sodium level was extremely low, they were going to send me to the hospital but I ended up not going. I took those lava salt tablets all day and was peeing normal. Had no problem holding any food or liquid down and felt okay. But when my family saw me they said I looked very bloated and that was true. I think I took in too much liquid that day and was not sweating enough due to the cool weather. (Horrible conditions). The symptoms I had were: weight gain, bloated look, low sodium level and towards the end of the race I was getting a little disorientated. I guess this is why the Dr. spent so much time talking to me and asking me specific questions. After researching this I found out that one can become hyponatremic (spelling?) and one symptom is disorientation. Also, the brain can swell in severe cases and lead to real problems. A few years ago a female runner in the Boston marathon died from taking in too much liquids. I have to really monitor what I take in next season since I am doing IMLP in July. I also think I took in too much liquid the days leading up to the race. Hope this helps a little, bob

## Hard Lessons Pave the Way

FROM: Fleet Subject: nice to sleep Monday, November 3, 2003 Morning awl...Traci...I never saw Wanda and of all the people I teach, coach and work with, I only saw my A.D., Teddy Frischling( one of my nyc marathon brothers and a good guy!) and his Dad on the course and 2 other teachers walking back to the gym after the race. Malcolm Fenton took some pictures and Maria Arellano flashed her beautiful smile which cheered me up...Yo el Grande Fella, thanks for the well wishes.... Anywho...I should have learned my lesson after the 60k in central park that it's a really bad idea to drive home after a race. The legs need to be moving for recovery and although I walked 2-3 miles back to the gym, took a nice long shower and had some more water, the trip home was a total nightmare I didn't expect traffic and of course I had to pee. The heart was trying to pump blood and all that crap out of my legs, while the liver was screaming from trying to process so much fluid. The saving grace was the second pee stop in which I walked around a bit before getting back in my car and then the traffic flowed and I got home. Karen nursed me back to health and my kids were quite adorable as they waited on me hand and foot. One thing I did different was to take a Tylenol 8 hour pain reliever, which I think helped the spasms in my calf, but leaves me wondering I almost popped some IB profin, but was afraid to combine or further tax the liver. I think that may have saved me from even greater distress on the ride home. I think this serious bonk yesterday was a good wake up call for the winter program that I will establish. Something has to work in creating greater flexibility; dropping some pounds and giving me a fighting chance to get safely back on the bike.

## Jenny II: The Maiden Voyage

The forecast was mid-forties, blustery winds and slight overcast. Despite partying like a rock star on Saturday night, I managed a solid performance at masters swim program and forged on to my final training mission of the week. Some guys at the club were discussing the proper clothing for their ride as I continued to come up with excuses for not riding. Once the guy mentioned that he goes out in 8-degree weather I was out of excuses. The weather, however, was not the only consideration. It was to be my first ride of the season and the first time riding this brand new, high tech, carbon- based, aero-bar end shifting machine, with a new set of clip-ins and frankly I was a little intimidated.

"Well, me and Jenny, twinklin' like crystal and pennies"... as I headed out onto the dreaded route 106. The wind was smashing us in the face, only this time my water bottles were actually heavier then the Red Kestrel Talon that promised to provide a smoother ride. I almost bailed at that moment, with the blistering cold rattling my bones and the elements threatening an early demise in this, my first voyage. I continued down the nasty highway, testing out the new gearing system located more conveniently on top as opposed to my down-tube shifters that I've grown so accustomed to using. Finally, I arrived at the service road and the wind blew me back once again. I slowly reached out and carefully rested my arms on the pads and reached for the shifters that were suddenly at my fingertips. I clicked the many gears that I now possessed and began implementing them to their fullest potential on the hills. What a joy to stay aero, maintain cadence and climb like an angel.

I committed the gearing system to memory so that it becomes automatic. Right a hand pulls up when climbing and left hand pulls up when it's time to put the hammer down. I approached some of my favorite passes and did just that, hammering down, knees bent inward, hands and arms tucked, head cranked in behind the gears and soared to almost 40 mph. This baby can move and I'm riding the dream machine. I backed off a bit, once I got that out of my system and re-focused on maintaining a safer ride as I continued to acquaint myself with my new suit of armor. I reached the turn- around at mile 20 and now it was time to suffer. The wind blasted me and I worked those gears to keep some, any kind of forward momentum. It didn't matter; there was only one-way home and no turning back at this point. Suddenly, a lone, hard-core cyclist on his Litespeed came out of nowhere and I knew I wasn't alone. He mentioned that I should lean into my bars on the uphill, but I contested his strategy. I reminded him that the smartest man in the world, a certain carpenter named Doug Fuller taught me to get off the bars and allow the energy and weight to be transmitted to the pedals. This strategy works for me and I've been quite successful. I conceded that with a blast of wind, and at the bottom of your ring, it's best to tuck and run rather then continue to allow the elements to push you around. We parted, wished each other safe travels and I finally found my way home. My darling Karen got some big time hugs and kisses as I felt like a new man out on the road and closed out the week with 14 hours of training which included 130 miles bike and one beautiful iron maiden voyage.

## Back Problems: A Letter from Scoot

March 1, 2004: Letters discussing back issues, nutrition and dreams.

Scoot, you know the story...back banged up from car accident and probably years of abuse, improper diet and too much of a gut. I've been watching the diet this time around as oppose to saying "with all this training I can eat what and when and wherever I want!" This year's ironman has some moderation. Focused on eating, but still enjoying my brew (although only the fancy stuff once in a while and the light brew to help cut back) and once in a while some rice pudding or ice cream. Still pretty hooked on chocolate and not really trying to break that habit. It just makes me so darn happy ;-)) Swim & running has been great! Swim has made me a new man and I really lean on this discipline to keep the stress off the body. Running has been moderate as a regular routine, with scheduled long runs put in there as I prep for LI marathon in 8 weeks. My approach is good this time w/much tri training carrying the bulk of improving cardio, but still feeling strong on my legs. The bike is getting better, although it's rare I can get off* without stepping VERY carefully as I put my feet to the ground and straighten up. Improvement from weight loss has been significant and serious occurrences of knees buckling from back spasms/pain is diminishing as I get in better shape. I am still quite concerned about those long rides coming soon and how paralyzed I will be when I'm done? I think I'm on the right track, but this is not an issue I ever dealt with in previous ironmans. I think the Kestrel w/ carbon has helped and there have been no episodes of real back trauma when clipping in & out as I had in the fall.~ I've been working pretty regularly (3-5 days/hr on the trainer) and getting out for 38-45 almost every week for about 6 weeks. Unfortunately, w/swim & run, I've abandoned the ab program and it may be the final missing piece?

As always, any suggestions are greatly appreciated! Fleet

Hi Fleet: I don't think ab work is the answer.~ I think exercises specific for the lower

back, and spine in general, are the answer.~ And I DON'T mean weights for the lower back.~ I mean flexibility exercises, including twisting, bending, knee rolling, and large exercise ball work, in combination with improving the biomechanical position of your lower back, depending on your structure shown on x-ray.~ If you have a loss of lower back curve, that requires certain exercises, and if you have an increased curve, that requires another.~ Of course, being a chiropractor, and working on people, including athletes, with lower back pain every day, ongoing chiropractic care may help improve your overall condition.~ Unfortunately you being there and me being here does not allow me to get into specifics, but most people benefit greatly when they do daily things to improve the health of their spine, just like we do daily things to improve our cardiovascular efficiency.~ Let me know if there is more that I can do.~ Focusing on eating healthier foods will always help you heal and stay healthy, with less pain. Scott

P.S. I eat chocolate too, but always dark chocolate, without any milk in it.~ Chocolate, although high in calories (so those that are fat need to abstain) has other benefits, including iron and antioxidants.

## Let it Ride

The work was done and the weather just right to knock down a personal best! I had some concerns because it was a long week with less sleep then I'm accustomed to getting and many obstacles including a late night 5th grade social on Friday that was quite stressful, household chores, marathon expo, party to work in the city. I was pleased the way things were going once I settled the boys down with some full court games on Friday, had a PR: 45 minute mowing early Saturday morning, followed by record breaking time in and out of expo with number, pair of Keyano's and plenty of time to get to the city. Party was a breeze, home to get the family to mass, settled in for traditional pre-race meal and off to bed.

Race morning was smooth to the start with juice, vitamin, slim fast and a bottle of water for the walk to the start. We picked up a guy going to the start whose wife couldn't drive him and he was psyched! Race went off moment after I arrived and the first 2 miles were at 7:15 pace! I began backing it off after realizing the company I was with, which included some Boston finishers and ultra runners. It was humid, but breezy enough to cool you down. I began singing John Hiatts' tune: " Im going down to Lincoln Town, turn your pretty little head around!" I decided to get rid of my hat and flung it up to a sign along the course. Hooked that baby and someone shouted "Nice shot!" Suddenly, I felt like Richard Dreyfuss in the movie, "Let it Ride" and I could hear the music kick in : "I got the horse right here his name is Paul Revere..." and at that moment knew that this was going to be a special day. I turned into Mitchell field shouting " Michael Johnson's got nothing on me!"

The miles were slipping away when I saw the "rat pack" running by and asked where the "Rudy" was on this fine day. Steve said that Aaron is where he always is, in the front of the pack! I continued to pull back, avoiding a blow up and a buddy of mine who had a 3:32 pr in Washington was running beside me. I flagged him down and then let him go as he was just doing the half. Finally I reached the split of full and half and turned it up a notch to the parkway. I was met with a stiff wind in the face, the quad burning kind and knew the rain would soon be blasting us. Sure enough, the storm hit, but only lasted a few miles. I drained my shirt under the bridge and reached the final turn-around with 7 miles to go. I was running with my friend Barbara from masters who finished in top ten of the women's division, but decided to let her go to avoid too early of a kick. The mood was outstanding, despite the wind that was supposed to now be at my back disappearing. At least it didn't shift and double me up, so I had that going for me. It was one final run around the park and I bust open my best time and get in under 3:30! With 2 miles to go, I needed to put together two 8- minute splits and it was time to get it on! I worked it all the way to the finish line, but didn't calculate the last .2 miles, nearly blew my calf and left it all out there. A 3:31ish time and next stop, Ironman USA!

## The other Side of the Bridge

"I can see clearly now, the rain is gone, I can see all obstacles in my way, gone are the dark clouds that had me blind, it's gonna be a bright, bright, sun shiny day, it's gonna be a bright, bright, sun shinin' day, yeah." It was indeed expected to be a clear blue sky, breezy and cool for our ride to Bear Mountain, but not that breezy and cool! Low 50's with an expectation of warmth later in the day guided my decision to stay with shorts and no extra clothing to hump around. Carmello, a buddy from swim masters program, met me at 4:30 a.m. and we departed to the city. Banged a spot, juiced up, got our gear from the gym and were on the road to meet C.C. Rider, fellow blue page peep, at the entrance to the park, as well as Luke, a guy I met riding in the park. We went a couple of blocks and Luke set the stage (and eventually the record) for pee stops on a ride, a record I formally owned. Thank goodness his riding capabilities overshadowed his need to relieve himself, or we could've been in for an even longer day then that which we were about to experience. All was well and we headed for Riverside drive to the George Washington Bridge. A reoccurring theme developed, however, as Carm's water bottles were not secured and would pop out of his cages. It was quite humorous the first time, as the bottle popped out, rolled gently across the city street, between the wheels of a taxicab, and safely to the curb. "Carm, your water bottles fell out!", later turned into, "Yo, get the frick back over here and pick up your own damn bottles!" It really wasn't the water bottles popping out as much as it was mile 75, many things on the trip were coming apart that compromised safety and an ability to get home and yet, we had to stick together, work as a team and finish strong.

We arrived at the George Washington bridge to meet Brian, a swim coach at Riverdale and the only other one, beside myself that has ever gone to the summit. All five of us, with a training mission to prepare for Lake Placid, joined at the hip and determined to conquer the mountain. CC Rider took the lead and I stayed close, knowing with these breezy, cool conditions and my longest ride to date being 66 miles in the flatlands, that I was going to be in for a long, suffer festival of a day. We made our first stop at the bakery in Nyack (mile 25), which is a haven for many cyclists, and then began to climb! CC's wheel wobble was still a problem which became more evident on the big downhill's and therefore, the caution flag came out and despite his hard efforts climbing, he would be forced to bring it all the way back throughout the day.

We arrived at Bear Mountain and worked our way to the summit on Perkins road, which is about 6 miles straight up! You basically must integrate some weaving and stair stepping out of the saddle techniques to get to the top. We decided that the trip back would be a different route, apparently more adventurous, great scenery and certainly more challenges then any of us anticipated.

The ride down the mountain is extremely tough on the bike, your body and the breaks, as you just hold on and keep the speed under control. I lost a bolt on my right brake lever, my handlebars shifted forward and adjustments were made when we reached the bottom. I tightened up the bars and actually moved them up a notch higher then the norm to make my position a little less steep. The break was still working, but there was cause for concern on the mountain. We went across Bear Mountain Bridge and directly into the face of the mighty bear! We climbed close to the edge, as the shoulder was quite limited. Suddenly, we were on a down hill slide, much like a roller coaster, but without a cable and no clue as to the next turn, dip or oncoming vehicle. I found myself going extremely fast and making maneuvers around turns that were way to close to the edge and circling wide into traffic! I slowly reeled myself in, pinching ever so slightly on the breaks to avoid flipping and talked myself down. "Easy Jimmy, easy!" "Slow the Frick down and get this baby under control!" Finally, I felt like I was in a safe place as a shot out of this slippery slope and began to climb across a magnificent landscape. I caught up to Brian, thanked him for one of the most spectacular rides of my life and then proceeded to smack him across the back of the head, reminding him that I've got a family that expects me home some time today!

It was all supposed to go well at this point until we found ourselves on the highway, with vehicles driving 70mph, merge lanes every 3-5 miles and "road hazard cut-outs/grooves" built into the road to awake sleepy drivers and in this case nearly break the moral of our entire group! We would have to cross these barriers from hell at least 10 more times before getting any relief. Despite my brand new, Vittoria, puncture proof tires; I was the first to fall fate to the dreaded flat zone. It was a good time to regroup, but just when the work was done, my 16-gram CO2 was overdone and POP! I changed the tire again, checking the interior and exterior, determining that it was a "snake-bite" which means the rim may have a defect or the tire was pinched upon instillation. We started out again and this was the point I mentioned earlier about Carm's water bottles flying onto the highway and my less then patient overtones somewhat expressed. We were all frustrated at this point, but I seemed to be shot out the back as my conservative refill left me with a maximum of 95 psi in the back tire, which did not thrill me one bit. I pulled over and grabbed one full bottle and slipped it into my jersey and then another, which I had to carry.

We made it to a town and one by one; the conditions from the treacherous highway reeked havoc on our group and dealt us a series of flats. The final leg of our ride was to be smooth sailing, but nothing could be further from the truth! The climbing wasn't over, the city limits were upon us and now we had some busy "hoods" to maneuver through which also included elevated train trestles, a maze of poles and a ground that cast a shadow, which did not allow you to see the monster pot holes that were just aching to grab hold of your already shattered body! Suddenly, the cramping began in my inner thigh and I could no longer rotate the pedal without severe cramping. I walked, stretched, drank more fluids which at this point was in excess of about 150 ounces which included, Gatorade, water, juice and a steady diet of power bars, slim fast, banana and nuts. Despite the cool conditions, I thought I fueled well throughout the day, but I think the amount of climbing against a stiff breeze fatigued the muscles to a much greater extent. The ability to ride in an aerobic state was diminished greatly throughout the day as we struggled to battle against a continuous wall of gravity and turbulence.

We reached a point in which our fearless and close to being strangled leader was departing from the group. The coach would dish up one more tasks before parting as if to say, if you can finish this training day you're all set for LP! I felt like Kiwi Kris because we now had to carry our bikes up a flight of stairs to get to the path like some adventure race. He saw that I was quite perturbed at this point and suggested I roll the bike along the ledge of the wall. This worked out nicely, but the profanity beneath my breath continued!

I reached the top, had difficulty clipping in and then both inner quads starting yanking my chain again! I lost the group, was out of fluids and thought I'd have to call a cab. I arrived at the top of the path and noticed a bridge above me, a road that went around an embankment, and a path that headed in the opposite direction. There was no way I was crossing the bridge and figured that was not the correct way because we already crossed the river at Bear Mountain.

I was just about to ride down to the highway and thought that I'd better pull back and be certain I'm going the correct way. Another cyclists pointed me down the cart path, explained that it will take me all the way downtown and that there's a guy with ironman USA jersey waiting for me. I was relieved that I waited, checked and then proceeded to walk down this very steep path instead of riding. I held onto the gridiron fence and inched my way to the bottom. I clipped back in and the pain in my inner quad persisted. I was so looking forward to this point when I could just spin home, but nothing would come easy on this day. I met up with the guys and asked them if they had any water. They pointed to the river and said, " There's your water Fleet!" I cracked a smile as the day was just about done and proceeded to grab Carmello's bottle full of Gatorade. I don't think he minded since I saved his bottles twice over the course of the day. And so my good deed paid off in the end as we spun our way back to central park.

A few tough uphills, some city busses and cabs and finally through the cart path and central park just hugged all of us! A good friend indeed is the park and when we arrived at the gym we had conquered 103 miles over some tough conditions and situations. It took us 6:49 in ride time and despite all the adversity and a slow time yielded on this trip, many new friendships, many hard training miles and so much to be thankful for was the result of this beautiful day. "Here is the rainbow I've been prayin' for, it's gonna be a bright, bright, sun-shiny day!"

## Bear Mountain II: Race Day Simulation

The preparation for the second trip to Bear Mountain this season included some bike tune-ups and a little tapering. I changed the saddle from Selle Italia to my old comfy specialized seat, tightened up the brake bolt that was lost on the last trip and put an emergency boot patch on the back tire that had a huge gash that was certain to cause trouble. My calf was tender and so I backed off all training leading up to the day. I did a full day of camp, a 2-hour birthday party and had very little sleep, waking up every hour until the alarm sounded at 4 a.m. We bumped up the time to avoid some of the heat, but by the time we departed from the east side at 5:35, it was already a humid 80 degrees and rising. The last tour was 50 degrees and freezing, so this was quite the switch.

My riding partners included CCrider/Tom, a real animal on the hills and a 45 year old, parent of one of my students named Frank, a German nuero-surgeon, under 5 hour Eaglman last weekend cycling extraordinaire! I knew I was going to get crushed on this day, but how hard was yet to be determined. By the time we hit the George Washington Bridge only 30 minutes into the ride, we were saturated in sweat and dehydrating at a fast pace. I steadied myself, choked down the second banana of the day to load up on potassium, tucked into my aero-bars and it was all business. It was a quiet ride with almost no conversation as we were all focusing on the road in front of us, and the pain that would most certainly be dished out! Most of the ride was uneventful, which was the goal for this trip based on the last disastrous tour on the opposite side of the river.

We climbed out of Nyack on 5th avenue up a hill that almost took some prisoners. CC's gears were skipping and when the car came up our back, the option to move left to right was gone and it was straight up! I experimented with "e" caps and thanks to CCRider, avoided the dreaded cramps in my quads that were a certainty based on the amount of climbing and continuous flow of perspiration that marked every mile of the course. It was such a thrill to be heading home on 9W, an old familiar friend, but the hills just kept smashing us in the face! They got steeper and more laborious with each encounter. The calf was pulling and all the Gatorade and "e" caps in the world weren't going to save this baby from blowing!

We spun hard in a flat windy section which precipitated the problem and suddenly I realized the company I was keeping and knew that if I was to get home safely, I needed to drop the gears and spin at a relaxed pace. Frank was beeped at about mile 80 and was called to the hospital in New Jersey. He gave me an encouraging smile and was off to do emergency surgery. It was a privilege to ride with Frank, but now it was time to get home. CC continued to inspire me and quite compassionate to my plight, feeding me with some more caps and supplying some much needed water. We arrived in the park at mile 100 in 6:18 which is a 12 minute p.r. from a previous year and although 2-3 miles less then our last excursion, was more then a half- hour faster! I attempted a brick around central park, but was quickly demoted to a fast paced 1-mile walk to and from the gym.

It was a great day on the mountain and a step closer to the finish line at Lake Placid. A final note places emphasis on pre-training day preparations and emotions that bring you to the day. Despite the comfy saddle change, the nose was little high for my comfort, but still worked well. The tire patch may have saved the day as I went "flatless" and the jury is not yet out on "e" caps, but if it helps to replace precious electrolytes, perhaps I can cut back on some of the fluids and be less bloated. I felt my best when the nutritional bars and drinks were absorbed and working their magic. On an emotional level, it's important that your training days consists of such challenges that put you in a relatively similar state of panic, excitement, concern as on the evening of race day. It will get you many more miles on the road to the ironman!

## Final Bear: One More for the Road

"...Ain't it funny how the night moves, just don't seem to have as much to lose, strange how the night moves." Final trip to Bear Mountain was quite uneventful and the way I like it! My doc friend, parent of two of my students, and person responsible for taking me on my first Bear Mountain ride, spanking me on every hill guided me through my final trip to the mighty Bear. Only this time I took the lead and never relinquished it (easy Lance), spinning up each hill with greater confidence. The plan was to go easy to the summit and pick it up on the way home. A little too easy for my liking, but a good decision given the fact that the race is in only 2 weeks! Tony tried to talk me out of going to the summit, but I would have none of that, chatting and smiling most of the way up and then dusting him in the final mile or so. "Is this a hill or a roller?" A hill is defined as one which requires climbing from a standing position while the roller allowed you to cruise 3/4 of the way up from the previous downhill. It became comical and cynical and painful as most were hills, but I called them rollers to maintain our spirits and motivation.

We finished the ride in 6:25, which included a 3:25 to the summit and just under 3 hours home without even hammering. A great negative split and plenty left in the tank to run a comfortable double loop of the reservoir (3 miler)..."These are the days of miracles and wonders, this is a long distance call so don't cry baby, don't' cry..."

## Taper Time: Post to Friends

I'm starting to like this taper stuff. I'm getting a lot of time with the family and getting excited about the race. In all this excitement, I forgot to mention some of the real important stuff. Karen and I are talking again after a one day stale mate since my last Bear Mountain trip. She wanted me to speak to some other ironmates to see how they feel, but no need; I already know what I've got. It's funny how tensions mount for both of us as the race approaches, only my darlin' has absolutely no control over the outcome and that can be much harder then us tapering fools. We are happily planning our calendar and putting together all the travel/final prep pieces.

Sunday, as the stale mate continued, my daughter Casey spun on a 2 wheeler for the first time :o She's a late bloomer like her father (didn't clip in until I was 35), but that little bit of magic was just enough to break the ice as two parents gleamed with pride :-) I found a good book (no, not a trashy novel,NTTAWWT), but a tri book by Matt Fitzgerald. I can now read about all the mistakes I've made leading up to the race :-( Actually, I've done some good things and the taper section of the book (along with the rain) is really helping me bring it home.

## The Race

The Aqua fit masters swim program provided an environment that forced me to work rather then slug along in the water. I finally learned how to swim after so many years of faking it in the water. Alternate side breathing and the ability to rhythmically breath with my stroke provided me with a greater ability to move comfortably through the water and save my energy for the remainder of the race. I still had to overcome my fears, inherent in a mass wave start, and come to grips with the fact that I was following the line again this year.

The cannon sounded and I delayed my start to allow all the maniacal swimmers to get going before attempting my swim. I ducked to the left side of the line as planned and began a relaxed, focused, smooth gliding stroke for the first loop. I encountered some body contact, but smiled, maintained my focus and cruised. It always helps to wave at the scuba divers that lurk beneath the surface and comforting to get a return "how do you do?" I had to remind myself to stay focused on the swim and not get too far ahead of myself in the race, as would be the strategy and philosophy throughout the day. I managed the second loop and finished in 1:17, which was 9 minutes faster, then my 2002 effort. Transition was slow and deliberate, as I know the day that lies ahead and wanted to properly prepare for a great ride. Despite my 13 minutes in T1, I was comfortable, relaxed and made a great decision to wear my vest. It was cold and knowing the downhill slide into Keene opted for the warmth and was less concerned about looking cool in my new color-coordinated jersey with Lance Armstrong insignia.

I began eating and drinking and taking the first round of e-caps, a nutritional supplement that provides you with the necessary amount of electrolyte replacement, without having to drink too many fluids. I wanted to race light and carry less weight throughout the day. I backed off on much of the food as well as the drinks and strategically finished my fluids prior to any/all of the big hills. This strategy worked well and is a direct correlation to knowing the course. I managed to get up the first set of hills and then noticed my right leg was bloody. It had already coagulated, appeared to be scabbing and actually looked pretty cool. I decided to continue on and deal with it later as the huge downhill to Keene was rapidly approaching. I was feeling great and took the hill like a champ. I arrived safely at the bottom only to discover a young lady was not so fortunate. Lying flat on her back and bleeding from the nose, I said a quick prayer and the medical assistants attended to her wounds. I later found out that she was transported by helicopter to the hospital and made a full recovery.

I was cruising along and saw some familiar faces. Mayor Woodman and Scoot were on the scene and I began my Doors rendition screaming "...when I was back there in seminary school, there was a person who put forth the proposition that you can petition the lord with prayer, petition the lord with prayer, petition the lord with prayer, YOU CANNOT PETITION THE LORD WITH PRAYER!"

Many smiles ensued from my friends and other riders. The Mayor commented on my fitness and prompted me to go for it! The first loop went well and the only problem came when I tried to turn right at the top of "papa bear" and another rider spaced out and kept going straight. I managed to maneuver the turn successfully and let him off easy. I finished in about 3:10, pacing well on the day with the goal being to "ride to the race" and when I arrived at the marathon it would be time to really go for it!

It was great to finish the first loop and see my family, as this would be the last time I saw them until the conclusion of the race. The second loop went beautifully until I arrived at Hazleton road. I was trying to make a decision about hammering it out on this section to manage a negative split or just cruise to enable a good climb back into town and a strong start to the marathon. I reached "the wall", a steep section on the course and suddenly experienced severe spasms in my inner quadriceps. My decision was made, but now a huge concern about my ability to even get back to Lake Placid, not to mention the remainder of this hill. I discovered to my dismay, that I had 2 gears remaining that should have been dropped. Grinding up the hill instead of spinning. A true rookie mistake, but hopefully not one, that would cost me my race.

I continued in a low gear and methodically spun all the way back. I had a nice chat with my friend Bob Cook, owner of The Runners Edge and responsible for hooking me up with wet suit, glasses, enduralytes and countless pieces of apparatus. I arrived in transition, completing the second loop in 3:20, a little shy of my even split, but quite acceptable considering the circumstances. It was a 6:33 total, which was about 30 minutes better than the 2002 race, and about 1:30 better then 2000. I spent my usual 10 minutes in transition that was once again deliberate to ensure a solid final portion of the race. I applied sunscreen, checked my hat, glasses, race # and sneakers.

I almost ran out of the tent when I realized I forgot my shorts. I like to wear the body armor liner and, well, thankfully noticed that I wasn't wearing the top shell. Once I got my pants on it was time to race. I was quite discouraged leaving town without seeing my family and each step down the huge hill was like being pile-driven into the concrete. I was hoping it would smooth out and the pain would eventually stop. I thought about walking numerous times, but continued to plow. Once again, I had to focus on this section of the race and leave all the other things behind. Continue to move forward and get to the end of river road. Once that section of road was complete, the arduous task of getting back into town would begin. When reflecting on the course that demanded this already on the bike numerous times, the task seemed more reasonable. The true test would soon come in the hills leading to the lake.

I was determined to run the entire way and so up the hill I went. All the way up the hill and at the top, a young spectator told me I looked better then anyone she had seen all day. This was a huge lift and I carried myself proudly into town. I blew past the special needs bag and happily headed past the lake. When I reached the zone that says "finish line", I played the little game most people play that are in good humor, shuffling between the two zones and then hanging the left and going back out of town. Only this time there was no pile driving affect and I let that hill roll me away for a final loop on the day. I made the turn on riverside and started reading the signs ... "Written in the letters of your name and brave the storm to come, oh it surely looks like rain."... Actually that little tune never played, with the exception of the folks at the end of the road that had a non-stop live Dead tape rolling. In fact, there were no hailstorms, no rain, no humidity, just sweet sunshine and a cool mountain breeze. I was down to 6 miles and all I had to do was run one more loop of central park in my mind and I was home free. In fact, this mental imagery drove me into town, unimpeded by hills, exhaustion or the daunting task of the long day. The sun was still shinning, no glow sticks, no spotlights, "no sleep, no light, no sound, so sleep, silent angel, go to sleep; sometimes, all I need is the air that I breathe and to love you." I saw Caryn, my torch bearing friend that DNF'd every year since 2000. I handed her my wristband with Tums and Advil and told her to get out there and finish this one. I later found out that she did just that in 11:28! I soared into the oval, picked up Casey and Amy and crossed the line in 12:40:25. It was 2:35 better then last attempt, 3:35 better then the race in 2000. I'm still waiting for someone to pinch me, wake me up and say "its race morning Fleet, good luck!"

# Race Week Excerpts

Race Week excerpts (in no particular order, rhyme or reason):

Hydration system: I've been using the profile handlebar system all season. On the day before the race, I had an opportunity to check out the run course on my bike, using for the first time a sponge in the hydration system to avoid overflow. It worked like a charm! I didn't spill any fluids. I did however discover upon my return a taste in my mouth much like when I was a child and used improper language. You guessed it, soap. I bought a sponge with detergent and luckily tested out my equipment prior to the race and made the adjustment for race day. Moral of the story: Test all equipment prior to race, don't try new equipment before race day and watch your language. BTW, Big Bear had nothing on me!

Pasta dinner & the Mayor: The food was it's usual pathetic offerings, but the entertainment provided by Mayor Woodman giving speeches, offering up race day for family of fallen child, and the usual selfless acts of Mr. Freese, PRICELESS! BTW, he actually asked me how many pounds I'd dropped, thanked me for the tunes and said I'd do ya, providing me with additional inspiration to move a little faster (No offense, Mayor).

The professionals: Joe Bonnes is my hero and conversations with him is always a thrill, especially when mentioning other fallen heroes like Garv and Lung and stories of down-tube shifting Pinarello's. Karen Smyers husband rocked the course and thought it was cool that his wife and son shared the same name as my wife and daughter. BTW, Karen has warned her husband that she's back in training.

Splash & Dash: My children symbolized ironman in all its greatness. On a small scale, I watched them fight through adversity, harsh conditions and become ironkids for the second time at age 8 & 5. We lost Casey's goggles, we lost one another, the rain came gushing in out of nowhere, Amy was afraid, Casey was scared, Karen was lost! Amy finally ventured into the water despite her fears, made it around the last buoy and brought it back to shore. Disaster struck a second time, as I was unable to leave one daughter for another. The rain came down harder and both children were crying. We finally got Amy running, but she went out too hard. She found herself on the ground, crawling and saying, "I'm tired, I'm tired, I'm tired! We managed to crawl a little and eventually cross the line. Moments later Casey ran into the oval, barefoot, soaked runner's shirt and a smile from ear to ear. BTW, so were Mom and Dad!

IBEX:The annual Beer exchange was at 8 p.m. at the beach. Fresh iron virgins included Snow, Beer Belly, Canironclyde, and seasoned veterans including oreoJo, schep, Uncle Terry, D-rock, scoot, Kinger, Sto, Johno, Aaron, CC.Rider, Burke & Jr. Eric, the Mayor, and some other visitors including Traci, Wanda, Chip, fastfreddie and others. I had the pleasure of playing the national anthem to open up the ceremonies and happily was encouraged to close with..."Little Red Rooster!"...BTW, one day I hope to play the banner in my wet suit on the peer to open ceremonies, jump off the peer and crank that baby!

Registration, Volunteers & Great Karma: Wicked Wanda and Babbs provide so much energy and service that allow a great day! One of the gentlemen checked me in and said "You're race # is 1130?" "Take a look at the clock!" It was 11:30 a.m.! If that wasn't enough, when I was in the oval, dressed in my wet suit on race morning, the announcement came over the loudspeaker: "1963 athletes registered for the 6th annual Ironman USA at Lake Placid". BTW, my age group is M40-44 and I was born in 1963!

Electric Avenue: The marathon course is always a special time for me in the race. I've got happy legs in marathons and thrilled when the issues of drowning or crashing are erased from the equation. It's important to note that in this race I experienced vibrations in my legs. It was a messaging and/or exhilarating feeling that came about any time I imagined or pictured something pleasant. I find it truly amazing how much power your brain has over the physical responses in your body. I need to further explore these trigger points in my brain that translated happy feelings into actual bodily healing. "Good God, we 're gonna rock on to electric avenue and then we'll make you higher!"

The Mass:    Saturday evening mass and the Ironman blessing from the entire congragation is always special. The communion hythm was one of my favorites and incredibly uplifting. I don't remember the tune, but do recall only the melodic sounds from the organ player. I was busting and had to let my voice be heard, when finally the pastor opened up the invitation to lyrical interpretation and I busted it out with tears in my eyes. Maybe someday I'll remember what song it was, but for now will settle for the memory of the feeling of peace and tranquility I received as a gift on the eve of the Ironman. . FLASH TO SUNDAY, SEPTEMBER 26TH: I gaze over at my daughters in the back row of the church, eagerly practicing the communion song at mass in anticipation of their debut in the choir next Sunday. A tear runs down my face as I'm transported back to Lake Placid as the girls sing... "I am the bread of life, he who comes to me shall not hunger...And I will raise him up, and I will raise him up, I will raise him up on the last day"

Celebration, C'mom! Three times a charm, so in my third year I managed to slip away to the Lake Placid Brew pub and have a few with the page peeps formally mentioned. Much fun and laughter was had by all. It was a pleasure charging the tab to Kinger, since he has a running tab. It was great to share stories of a day gone wild! In closing, I jammed out many tunes for Lyle Harris the program director. I was asked to do the national anthem at the volunteer party the next night, but family had to come first. BTW, I will play for you guys on that pier one day!

Bear Mountain revisited: The mighty Bear proved to be the best training ground again, capable of flattening out even the toughest slopes in Lake Placid. Much thanks to CC. Rider, Mello, Brian, Frank, Luke and my mentor Tony Squire that's been there from the beginning. BTW, next time it's 5 trips up Perkins road.

Jenny I, Jenny II & Karen: It was Christmas morning and a star was born. I count my blessings every day for the family I have and the love I've received. My darling Karen continues to shock and awe me with her generosity, support, and continuous inspiration as she busts open the budget and hooks me up with sweet carbon. Jenny the Pinarello was with me in Lake Placid in spirit, Jenny II, the Red Kestrel Talon carried me safely to the final bike transition and Karen carried me home in her heart!

# 2006 Ironman Triathlon at Lake Placid: "Unplugged"

## Introduction '06

"Well this will be the last time, this will be the last time, maybe the last time I don't know?" I've played that tune a few times in my mind, and as mentioned in one of my final reports, I'm in a brotherhood, a club, a "Cult of Personality!"

The return to Lake Placid and the year leading up to this monster event brought with it dramatic scenes and a poetic conclusion. The tears of laughter and joy flowed endlessly as I closed out one of my toughest years in training that carried with it many others of life's challenges. The race is just one day, the battle in life is continuous as a constant attempt to improve one's performance professionally, socially, emotionally and make my family proud! The story lines are consistent with previous years, in which I hope to relay a feeling to the listener that I walk tall, proud and carry a song in my heart that I only wish all that I come in contact with can hear. I'm human! I trip, I fall, I get knocked down and then I get up again, thrilled to be alive and be able to do what I do and hopefully do it well!

# Long Island marathon '06

# 8605 FROM: Fleet Subject: quickie race report Sunday, May 7, 2006 01:52 PM Host: ool-44c259c4.dyn.optonline.net

Most beauteous day, perfect for a pr, held 8's comfortably through 20 with insurance minute or two, all smiles, great tunes (first time ipod) and the blew up at around 24, hobbled home with a 3:49ish...got over confident yesterday with pr on a 40 miler with new Zipps and a brew or two at communion party which may have cost me my race. Oh well, got's me some major wonderful blessings in my family and next stop...Lake Placid

## Weekend at Jimmy's

"Dyin', cheatin', hurtin', that's all ya seem to do! Messin' around with every guy in town, puttin' me down for thinkin' of someone new! Always the same, playin' your game, drive me insane, troubles gonna' come to you! This is all I wanna' say to ya women, your time is gonna' come!" I cranked the tune louder, all smiles upon my face. The first trip to Bear Mountain of the season complete and despite a couple of kinks in the road, it was a pretty safe trip. Suddenly, out of the corner of my eye, I noticed a guy on a motorcycle attempting to split me and another car next to me. Before I could even finish my thought process of how insane this guy was going 75 m.p.h., I heard a thud, looked in my rear view mirror and witnessed the most horrific scene. The guy hit the pavement, rolled numerous times, cars swerved to avoid hitting him and the other guy on a motorcycle was attempting to quickly dismount and rush to his aid. I must have traveled another mile before I could actually comprehend what happened. It was at a tricky section of highway in which the road divided, and became a six-lane section and there was no chance of turning around. I reviewed the situation in my mind a thousand times before reaching my final destination. Why would he do that? Did he bounce off my car? Is he okay? The questions continued, the fears of fatality on the highway rushed through my head and the emotions overcame me, as I got angry, confused and then sobbed.

I arrived at our friend's house and began to describe the scene. My wife and friends comforted me and assured me that there was nothing more I could have done. I had spent the entire day, traveling to the city and methodically tailoring my way up riverside drive, across the hair-pin turns of the George Washington Bridge, scaling a repeated on slaught of hills, conservatively working the down hills and paying special attention to the action all around me. I once again put myself to the task and questioned every part of my being. Is this too close to the edge? Is vanity the greatest sin? We push ourselves to get in the best shape of our lives and search out bigger and more challenging experiences, while making every effort to get home safely. We can't control the traffic, the weather, and the animal that charges across our path, but we can continue to take every precaution to increase the odds of getting home safely. And yet, the controversy and guilt continues to make me uneasy as I question those facts and ask myself, are you doing everything possible to get home to your family in a safe manner?

There were questions raised about the beautiful, most prestigious wheel set under the sun that my lovely wife gave me the green light to purchase. The sweet carbon will ensure a smoother ride, which translates into a healthier, happier, more productive husband at the conclusion of any ride. I didn't need the hard sell tactic, as Karen wants everything that is good for me and along with my children, she is my greatest inspiration! No, the questions came after I made the investment. Those wheels are just for racing! That wheel set can be pretty hairy in the wind with 81mm of depth! They will only hold up a few seasons if you ride them all the time! I immediately addressed the questions of duration on these babies and as always appreciated the feedback I received from my wife and friends. I'm convinced that the theory, which states clearly and unequivocally that you need to train with the equipment that you race must be the prevailing factor when making the final decision. It goes without question that I need to continue to work on hills, in windy conditions and figure the safest and best way to handle these babies in practice conditions. The plan is to continue to follow lessons learned in previous years, once again to map out the safest and most efficient way and enjoy the journey! In an effort to be somewhat conservative, I will swap out my old wheel set in the odd years when not racing. This response was practically a "no brainer", which brings me back to the question, is vanity our greatest sin? I'm convinced the new wheel set provides a smoother ride, but the number of times I've grabbed the steering, tightened in the gut, and prayed for mercy may be too many times already. I've learned a few tricks to help stabilize the bike, including slowing down, raising slightly upward to create better balance, a "no aero-bar policy", and total concentration and an awareness of the windy conditions. I'm still searching for answers and perhaps I always will, continue to question my path and the map that I am following.

The trip to Bear Mountain, especially the first ride of the season is always dramatic. In previous years, I've made the mistake of being under trained and suffered for my lack of preparation. This would not be the case, as I already banked two local centuries, three 80 milers, a couple of 66ers, a truck load of 40 milers and a descent marathon finish which was more in the category of a training run given the volume of training leading up to the event. However, my entourage would not be so well prepared and the suffering would soon begin!

We planned to depart an hour later to avoid any lingering showers and as a result avoided a major "pea soup" type fog that only thickened as the road turned north. The sun gave way, dispersing the fog and any concerns of impending rainstorm. The pace was slow, the group got separated as Brian and I picked it up a notch! I recall Brian saying, " I hate myself every time I take this trip!" Although I shared his sentiments, it is a necessary evil to prepare for race day. We made a stop and when there was no sign of our partners, we realized that someone got a flat. Once again, the pace was slower then was acceptable, but I knew how much more work was to be done and remained patient. We finally regrouped, but it wasn't before long that we forged on and worked our way to the top. Tony and Ed had already decided that they were not going all the way to the summit, so it was a race to the top! Brian earned the king of the hill title, but would later be dethroned and stripped of his title on the day as he bailed out of 9W and took the flatter section back to Nyack.

Tony, my main man, chief surgeon of Mt. Sinai hospital, and my first Bear Mountain partner, raised the ante and started smoking those hills on the way home. He would later pay for his insolence as the cramp monster jumped out and bit him before he could get home. We met up again in Nyack as a group and the plan was to take the flat route home. Sure enough, another flat and no 650 c spare. We patched it and then picked up the pace for the final surge to the bridge. What goes down must go up! We managed to avoid a slow, death crawl up hill, but were now faced with a steep, four tier section that can most certainly take claim to anyone unprepared. We worked to the top and the sight of the GW was pure bliss. Tony cramped on the way home and after a few enduryltes, and a quick drink stop, we found ourselves on the victory path of central park.

I had plenty of fuel still in the engine and geared up for a 7-mile brick of central park. Learn that poem, learn that poem, learn it! It was nice to see two of my athletes from our track team, one in particular that was the mile and 800 champion in the ICAHN Stadium Final Games. Somewhat symbolic and inspirational to have my top endurance athletes from a team of 40 show up at the entrance to my stomping ground. It was the first time in many attempts to do the entire 7-mile loop after a Bear Mountain trip and helped to close the day in solid fashion!

I awoke the next day, excited about spending the day with the family, moving the trampoline, putting up the pool and saying goodbye to some old dear friends. The rhododendron, once dubbed the "purple monster" with its' magnificent flowers, met its' match with the emergence of a line of maple trees that seem to say "ain't no sunshine when she's gone!" Prior to this initial burst on the day, I looked for front-page news, on line information, anything to clue me in on the previous days motorcycle accident. No news is good news and a new day has dawned. The removal of my old pal went well, and we had the entire family re-locating the trampoline from the space that is designated for the pool. When we uncovered the intex special that survived three full seasons, we discover numerous holes in the bottom. None that can even compare with the holes in my daughters hearts and their summer pool fantasy was quickly dashed and disappointment rang true on their frowning faces. Casey and Amy were not to be denied and as luck would have it, the local store had a bigger, better model and we were back in business. Okay, so bigger is not always better as the space, which we allotted and the leveling work completed, just became another project. Fortunately, the retainer wall was already in place and some quick reinforcements to a section, paved the way for miles of smiles. A great way to spend the day as the ice cold water that began filling the new summer dream provided for much needed therapy to this old man's broken down legs!

There was still one more day, a recovery ride, trip to grandmas and final touches on the pool set up. In short, I blazed through a 56 miler, as Long Island roads are a welcomed sight after conquering the mighty Bear! Hills become mere speed bumps and the lay of the land is well known. I had to call it quits a little sooner then expected as my quads were cramping from the heat, and a desperate dash for an outdoor bathroom facility in a local park helped save the day. I'll skip those details and let's just say I made it safely home. And yet, "safely" takes on, yet an entirely new meaning, but always continues to be the driving forces behind all my rides.

## Bearing Down Gearing Up

The Final Bear Mountain trip was on the calendar and unlike any of these rides; it was a sleepless Friday night. There's just no getting around the drama inherent in a 100 mile ride that sends you through the mean streets of Manhattan, across the George Washington bridge, scales up a narrow shouldered, sand and pot-whole ridden highway and some of the nastiest elevations in New York! It's quite possible that if this was all one had to contend with, the result could then be one of an individual that is well rested and prepared for the long haul. Unfortunately, this year alone has brought with it other obstacles that plays tricks with your mind and leaves you on the defensive before pedaling that first mile.

Although the first two trips went extremely well, there was a definite underlying presence and feeling that kept me on guard and a little on edge for this final push to close out the season's training. In the first trip, we managed a descent pace on the ride and I was able to do a 7-mile run around central park for the first time in 5 previous futile attempts. I was all smiles on the drive home, when I witnessed in my rear view mirror a motorcycle attempt to split me and another car going 90 mph and BAM! He didn't make it and my sense of security on a safe day was gone! It was a little close to home and although it had nothing to do with my trip to Bear Mountain, it got me thinking. The next trip was scheduled 3 weeks later and I was pleased that this ride went without incident, but that's not to say there wasn't some underlying drama built into the ride as we headed for the summit. It was this same weekend that a women plunged to her death in her car over the very same peak in which we proudly look out over at the top of Perkins road. The story was extremely sad and I offered up all my suffering on that day to the family and those children strapped in their car seats that will never be the same. The children survived the crash; the husband was questioned on murder charges or the possibility of an aided suicide. Needless to say, it was a rather dramatic weekend and my thoughts and prayers go out to this family and all those that are affected by violence and depression in their lives.

And so, the final trip begins and all is well. I find a spot in Manhattan, follow my routine and head up Riverside Drive to the bridge. I meet a guy with a European accent and as it turns out, he is also going to Bear Mountain and doing Lake Placid. I thought it was strange when he told me his name; it wasn't Franco or Stefan, but Sam. We arrived at the bridge and the gate to cross was locked! We figured the recent terrorist plots uncovered in NYC prompted the Mayor to lock down passages across the bridge. I attempted to call my friend Brian that accompanied us on the previous two trips and is a major inspiration in my training pursuits, but my service was dead. Sam made some calls with no luck and we proceeded to venture to the other side of the bridge to make our crossing. We carried our bikes up a flight of stairs and managed to ride across the bridge, maneuvering around the trestles until we reached another set of stairs. We quickly learned that going down the stairs was much more challenging and required a certain amount of confidence, some of which I had none! By the time we reached the other side my quads were burned and my entire body tense from bracing for a fall. The medal grid like stairs were steep and there was concern of either slipping or getting my cleat caught inside the ridges of the stairs. " Is this the way it goes down, I crash on a set of stairs across the George Washington Bridge?" " But I'm an Ironman, and this can't stop me!" We made it safely across, met up with the rest of the crew that included Charlie from Tennessee that would eventually prove he could climb like an angel and was on his 5th straight race at LP! Immediately, I felt my quad tightened, but lead the pain train for about 20 miles of the ride. It wasn't before long that I was shot out the back and chased the pack all the way to the peak. Sam made a quick exit at Perkins rode, the beginning of the 3-mile grueling ascent to the peak and

I forged on, attempting to save some face on this slippery slope of the mountain. A couple dudes flew by on the way down; assuring me that my friends were waiting and when I arrived it was all good! I'd reached the top; worked hard to get there for a 3rd time this season and it was time to go home. A couple of "Harley dudes" from Elmira were there and admiring our bikes. Brian had the custom Trek with Cosmo elite wheel set and truly an impressive ride. Charlie had a pretty standard Trek set-up. But it was Jenny, the beautiful Red Kestrel, with the brand new 81 mm deep rim zipps that caught the biker's eye and like a proud papa Bear on the mountain, I grinned and took that baby home!

We move pretty good with the wind at our backs, but the quad burning, stair climbing, and wind in our face all the way up was starting to take it's toll. I knew I had a few more serious hills to go and started slamming endurolytes like m&m minis, which ironically enough is the container in which I store them. It all went well, but the final, four- tier, steep climb in Englewood was still ahead and I was in trouble. I stair climbed it all the way home and prayed the bridge was open. Save your prayers buster as the sign read "CLOSED FOR CONSTRUCTION UNTIL SEPTEMBER". I was relieved that terrorism did not play apart in the bridge closing, but 90 miles later and we are back to humping our bikes across the bridge and now the challenge has tripled. I gripped tightly on the rail and one-stepped it all the way down. There was no way I was going to fall down this flight of stairs. Made it safely across, down riverside drive and into the park for final 4-mile ride. Usually the park hugs me, but today I found myself trying to push the final stretch only to be frustrated by roller bladders, runners, carriages, pedestrians and a massive crowd! I reached 5th avenue, shut off my odometer that hadn't worked all day and reminded myself to be careful in city traffic on the streets. I cruised to a stop at the Guggenheim museum and as I attempted to cross, was halted by another cyclists in my path that wasn't moving. I attempted to put my foot down; not realizing that I was clipped in and down I went! People rushed to my side to block oncoming traffic and make sure that I was okay. I was embarrassed, angry and pumping my fist at the guy that stood still, but the reality was that after 100 miles of riding, it was my bad. The gorgeous Brazilian women that offered me comfort and attempted to help me with my bike was a sight for sore eyes, and legs and back, but really made me feel good about the responsiveness of people and how quickly people are willing to help. With just a skinned knee and minor bruises on my arm, I packed up my bike and geared up for a run around central Park. I wanted to test out a Desoto shorts and pants outfit to improve transition and the comfort level was outstanding. The heat was a little much, but I managed a solid 7 miler and put this training to rest! Next stop...Lake Placid, Ironman USA!

# Unplugged

I always have a difficult time with taper week and this part of our race preparation. No more big miles to burn those calories; keep off the weight, and the nervous energy builds. We review in our minds the countless hours spent training, quality days in the saddle and the mega-miles we accumulate to get to the start, all the while living close to the edge and keeping a watchful eye of our injuries. The bike is carefully checked and race tires are mounted. We plan out every step trying to control as much as possible to be successful. When all that is done that can possibly be managed, it becomes a waiting game as we observe, monitor and deal with those things out of control. The children are bickering, the kids we care for on certain days show up with an extremely contagious virus and those things that are off the scale in terms of predictability begins to creep into our lives. It is at this point that we must calmly handle these situations and avoid the pre-race blow up! We carefully defuse the children that are arguing and gently call our friends to come get their children.

The week turns into a month and all my defenses are out as I continue to turn myself inside out and try to anticipate any other problems that might influence getting to the start line. We inspect the Jeep, change the tire, pack our bags and hit the road. Finally some relief as we get through the tricky sections of our trip and arrive at route 87 that takes us to Lake Placid. Suddenly the rain comes in a torrential downpour and we decide to put the Jeep in "part-time"! We are 30 miles from Albany at 6am and the Jeep now sounds like a demo derby with over churned engines and ripped out mufflers. Strangely enough, I had a sense of relief as one of those unpredictable moments occurred and it was time to overcome the first real test of adversity. The implications of a breakdown sets into motion a brand new plan that will affect registration, the kid's race, warm-up swim around the Lake and suddenly the pace for race preparation becomes furious! We stopped at the next place on the road and there was no service. I tooled around with the 4-wheel drive and the gears magically snapped into place! We were on our way and Lake Placid seemed closer, brighter and bigger then ever!

Once we arrived I could feel the steam pouring out of my body! We had made it and it was time to do final preparations for Sunday's race. Registration went smooth as the kids went swimming prior to our room being ready. It was all good as we prepped for the kid's race. In previous years I did not realize how much pressure the children feel for their race and was prepared to make the transitions comfortable for them. No more "floaties" in the water and this year Casey was being sent down the road for the full mile! I jumped in the water with Amy and did a back float for the length of the course to assure her safety. We got out and blew through transition skipping the sneakers and shirt and blasting up the hill. Amy is a powerhouse and insisted on going faster! She placed fourth over-all and was all smiles. I jogged to the other side of the lake, slapped on my sneakers and geared up for Casey's descent from the water. She came out and ran half way down the street with her goggles on in pure "Casey-esk" form. She worked hard and asked me how I do it! She never complained and showed a lot of guts on the course. She finished strong and was proud of her accomplishments!

It was now time to take a loop of the swim course and everything was going according to plan. I experienced some body contact, which was really strange with so few people in the lake. It was mild contact as the guy next tome was fighting for the line? I had a good laugh and after a brief chat with a couple planning for next years race, managed a 40-minute loop. I packed up my wet suit and my family arrived and picked me up in a rowboat. It was joyous and delicious and things were really smoothing out!

We cleaned up, had some dinner and headed for the beach for the annual IBSEX (International Beer and Scotch Exchange) with all the blue page peeps. 7 years since we all met on a web page in cyber land and it is quite the cozy gathering. Mayor Woodman in his 8th consecutive LP appearance and 17th Ironman was on hand to lead in the ceremonies. In attendance included Scoot, Banger, Kinger, Big Fella, Oreo Jo, Crazy ultra Paula, Schep, Uncle Terry (and the pups), Burke, Barbarian, Brian, Justfred, and Jepphany. Although only a handful of peeps would be racing, the support was incredible and there was still another entire contingency of folks that would make up Garv aid 3 miles out on the run course. We would later see Latrick, Johno, and of course Garv! It was time to pack it in as we had been up since 4 am and tomorrow brought some more race day preparations.

The plan was to check my bike and do a test ride of the run course. It's about 13 miles, which gives you some perspective of how far out of town the run course is and the steepness of the hills. Going out the back puts you on the bike course and you get to feel mamma bear and pappa bear's wrath that concludes the race. The rain is trickling down and the concerns about the weather creeps into my mind. I return to the hotel room, finalize my transition bags and stall my trip to the oval as it's now pouring outside. I decide to pump my tires one last time and discover a flat! The faulty valve reared its ugly head on my short practice ride! I suddenly had… "a peaceful, easy feeling and I knew nothing would be getting me down, because I was already standing, on the ground!" This was some wonderful Karma that swept me off my feet and carried me through the night. The rain was pouring, we were all getting soaked as we abandoned our bikes in the oval for the massive bike sleep over and it was all good! "Let it rain, let it rain, let your love rain down on me!" The next day was race day and it was going to be gorgeous.

Race morning finally arrives after an evening of nightmares that wakes you up every hour on the hour. Although I slept reasonably well, the visions of missing the start of the race, crashing on the road to Keene and bonking on the run leaves me exhausted. The cold, dark, threatening sky of the mountains is intimidating and the rehearsal of positive, and inspirational lyrics is an attempt to drive away my fears. "Wake up to find out that you are the eyes of the world…"! My wife is by my side once again on race morning and although Rocky prescribes to one method before a major prize fight, I have a different approach and it helps to keep me calm throughout the morning and well into the day. I head down to the transition area and drop my bags. I walk with my friend Daryn from Long Island that I did my first century ride with back in April. We part and wish each other good luck! I see my training buddy Brian that I took 3 trips to Bear Mountain with and he's always a bright sight! Schep is there with marker in hand, marks me up and puts Fleet on my opposite calf. I inspect my bike and then run into Oreo Jo. She asks me if I figured out my costume and given the coldness on the day, I go with changing completely into dry cloths out of the swim and ditching the sleeveless. I try to break the tension, as I sense some real nerves, and ask Jo if it's frowned upon to be intimate with my wife on race morning? She grins and of course, totally agrees with my philosophy. I arrive at the water and Burke is there to greet me. We make our way into the cold, dank lake and the tension is thick! I feel slightly overwhelmed, but there is no turning back!

The cannon sounds and I wait for the maniacs to go. I creep along the dock, slip out to the left and begin to stroke. I'm amazed that I have the lake to myself. I really exaggerated my move left this year, but knew I would have to get back in the thick of it to get around main buoys. It seems like an eternity, but I keep stroking, find myself directly on the line and being swept along with the field. I take a few hits and go back to the left where it's quiet! Around the first set of balloons and it's breast stroke time. The field did not prescribe to my method, so I lowered my head, stroked violently to a clearance and re-established my breathing control. I looked for the scuba guys that always calm me down, but the water was too murky. Came out of the water in 37 minutes and I feel great! One loop to go and my feet will be on solid ground. Limited contact as I went stroke for stroke with one identifiable wet suit and it worked like a charm. I was out of the water in 1:15 with my best time and off to get stripped!

I begin my run to the oval and my brother Tony that came from Florida with his family was screaming, "Jimmy, Jimmy, look at the camera Jimmy, wave to the camera!" This went on all day and I have the best footage of this race ever as Tony refused to lose, battling the crowds and working the production! I arrive in the tents and it's more crowded then I'm accustomed to from my previous races. Usually it's a more relaxed group after the 1:20 mark, but I was in a more competitive setting. I carefully gathered my clothes, geared up and headed out. It's a great moment when you get to your bike and survive the swim, but Keene Valley is the next dreaded spot after humping over the first set of hills by the ski slopes. It's raining, I can't see through my glasses and the roads are slick.

I remove the glasses and begin to force feed food and fluids. The plan is to ride to the race. I know all too well about blowing up on the first loop, and with the rain I have no intention on exiting this race from a crash. Perhaps a tad too conservative, but I know energy conserved on the bike translates to the run, which is a much safer place to hammer! The hill to Keene is wet and nasty. People are pretty conservative and doing the right thing. I stayed well within my speed comfort zone which does not allow greater then 40 miles an hour and much less on the wet roads. When I arrived at the bottom a guy with a sleek time trial helmet says to me "Thanks for slowing me down or I would've ate it on that hill!" I wasn't sure if he was angry with me, being sarcastic or sincere? I realized that he was truly grateful and must have been following my cues down that hill. It felt great to finally have that one behind me and as the day went on and the more difficult tasks were behind me, I could feel myself getting stronger!

I arrived at special needs bag, snatched it up on the move, made the right turn at the lake and began searching for my family on the left side. We didn't talk about it, plan it and it was one of those things that just fell into place. There they were, with the sun shinning, all dressed in shirts with my finishers photo plastered on their chests that read "Go Jim, Go and Go Daddy Go" I was somewhat oblivious to the gesture, yelled at my wife to get my food out of the bag and yes, it's all caught on tape! I kissed and hugged everyone and despite my wife's plead to get out and race, I must kiss my girls before going back on that mountain. It was cold, so I kept my vest, pedaled up the hill and realized how very lucky I was. I raced through the town and saw the Frederick family that live in Saranac Lake. They were at the race in 2000, my first grand debatuary; nearly midnight finish and provided great support! It was nice to see that they moved back and were once again at my side!

The second loop is always so sweet as it's the last of the over 2000 miles and 7-century rides that I would endure. I prepped well for the bike, but true to form on Hazelton road, things started coming apart. I was actually going for it and hoping for a possible even split. I busted down one hill trying to max out the momentum and spin out of the saddle in the same high gear going up. My quad folded, spazzed-out and once again, as in the previous year, I was reduced to a low gear spin all the way back to Lake Placid with major concerns for blazing a trail on the run. I popped my e-caps like the M&M minis, which they were housed and continued to hydrate. I did the math and thought I was closing the deal with a solid performance. With each hill and continuous urge to relieve myself, my time was suffering. Marshals were everywhere and there was not a porta-poty in sight. I found myself going off the road behind buildings to avoid a strike and put my personal record on this course in jeopardy. It's a 4-minute penalty, which is assessed physically in a tent on the course. I knew this was going to be huge for the final outcome in terms of a P.R.

My friend Daryn was in sight and informed me that he was stung multiple times by a bee that was trapped in his helmet and also had a gash in his finger. He was hurting, but I could not provide much support and began to get concerned about a drafting penalty as we road side by side. I pulled off the road again to pee and later passed him at Papa Bear. I later found out that he did not make it on the run and those uncontrollable factors that creep up and cause so much mental fatigue leading up to race day was showing itself in Live color! I pushed away the demons and blasted to the finish line. Once again the family was there to greet me, but my youngest daughter was sound asleep. She had strep and hung tough all day. I quickly changed and got out of transition in 6 minutes after a somewhat disappointing 6:45 bike split. I saw my family one last time and to my wondering eyes, zoomed in on Amy that was awake and as beautiful as the day was long! Tony prompted me to wave to the camera as I headed out to the marathon course. I did the math and my sub,12 hour day was out of reach! I knew I had much work to do and my pr was still a great possibility. I stormed down the hill using every ounce of momentum that the hill would provide, while being certain not to trip!

The road leveled off and I began to find my stride. Garv aid was around the corner and the boys picked me up and sent me out for my final run. I banged over 600 miles in six months following an ankle sprain falling off a ladder in late December. Meg the athletic trainer at work was a tremendous help to my recovery and her support is greatly appreciated! I ran one marathon, did four 19 milers, cranked 26 half marathons on a hilly central park, a truck load of 7 milers and was not going to be denied! I managed the first loop in 2:06 with the "no stop running" plan, which included every hill. The multiple porta-potty stops did allow me to read my heart rate and cool off a bit, but then it was back in step.

My family did not estimate my time and missed me leaving town for the final loop. I was okay with that, as I had to buckle up for a strong finish. Once again I passed Garv aid, ditched my hat, glasses and all my emergency supplements, which included some Tums and Advil. I held on to my caps and continued a combination of iced over cups of Gatorade throughout the course. I ate like a champ on the bike which is always a necessary chore and my only responsibility on the run is to moderate my drinking (what else is new☺! I cranked it up a notch as I passed my friend Brian. He asked if I was on my second loop and suggested that at this pace I would be in at 12:45. I decided that would be unacceptable as my previous finish was a 12:40 and I was too close to break that mark.

I felt strong, sang a song, and worked my way to the end of the road, which put me into my final, rhythmical, last central park run of the year. I don't look at miles, I only think about it being my last run! I clear my head of all the dread and pretend that I'm just starting my one run for fun. The hills will have nothing on me and I will pace all the way home!

There was a girl lying down in the woods at the edge of the road and she had bonked pretty bad! Thank goodness emergency help was readily available and says a lot about the professionalism of this organization that handles this race! She was in good hands and it was time to bring it on home!

The clock was ticking and I was closing in on my record. I knew how long that Mirror Lake run was and lifted the pace again. I made the final turn, with arms extended to mimic the wingspan of a plane and began to lower my landing gear. That shit-eating grin created ripples and dimples in my face the size of craters as I checked my watch and knew I was all the way there!

I sped into the oval searched for my kid cargo and as they excitedly jumped out onto the stage, we clasped hands and bolted to the tape!

"Smiling and waving and looking so fine"… the emotions took over! A 12:37 finish and with a 4:18 marathon I managed to break my course record by a hard fought 3 minutes and 15 seconds!

There are always so many people to thank that help us arrive safely to the start of this race and put up with our year long selfishness as we leave the family to train and then arrive home shot. We look great, get stronger, but can't do it alone. Is this the last one? Are we willing to follow a plan that gets you to the start line and finish in dramatic form? Does the pressure become greater each time or am I just trapped in the moment?

It's definitely not the last one as I'm in a brotherhood of hard working, driven people and this family will always require a reunion that includes me in the thick of it! Although my plan is solid as I have been consistent in my last two attempts, there is great concern with the path I feel I must take. Bear Mountain leads the way for my biggest fears. Manhattan, George Washington Bridge, 9w, Haverstraw, the narrow shoulders, the big trucks, the steep downhill's. And yet it's my greatest tool that provides all the necessary elements to prepare you for race day. The sleepless nights that are inherent because it is such a dramatic, technical day ahead. The huge strokes to the summit and the uncertain return with the constant threat of bonking! The 7 mile run around central park and the uncertainty of it all!

The pressure does become greater as more time is invested, more money sifting from a family budget for better equipment, higher gas prices, hotel and race fees escalating out of proportion and the sheer popularity of a race that starts over 2300 people in the water! The race sold out in 90 minutes and the demand for this race is so great, it is just one more thing that is going to be out of or control! And so, it's time to learn or little lessons, digest them for future years, enjoy that which can never be taken away and have faith in those things we cannot control. Peace love and joy to all those that have been there! Most importantly to my darling wife Karen, my daughters Casey, and Amy that provide me with so much love and inspiration and have carried me to my 4th Ironman finish!

# Local Events Revisited

PT. LOOKOUT LOCAL TRI '05

The swim will never be easy. The horn blew by surprise and my goggles immediately filled with water. The waves were smashing me; I was slamming into bodies everywhere (243 person mass start). Fixed my goggles and on my way. Thought the sweep was much stronger and turned at 1st buoy only to run into the pack and realize I still had the entire course to go. Alternate side breathing was out, more body contact and no pace. Finally settled in and got home. Saw the family and got some help from tri-coach unzipping wet suit. (21:40 3/4 swim and T1) Tough early going on the bike into stiff wind and eventually picked it up and starting passing peeps. Moved well on the course, some tightness in the back, but manageable. (29:00 10 bike including T2) Difficult start on run as breathing has been an issue lately. Slugging around too much weight for these sprint races. Finally got it going, joked with a guy about getting water from the littlest of volunteers and starting passing people. Put a big Bulls eye on the back of my buddy Richey who lifeguards at the pool in the city. Really didn't want to live down a loss all winter long in my own backyard. Chased him and 12 others around the final turn. I caught most of them and dropped my buddy in the final stretch. I asked him if we were going to let 2 girls beat us and he prompted me to go ahead. Came up on a guy that clipped me at the tape last year and put it into full throttle! He lost his goggles at the swim start and that would've been quite the demoralizing loss and so I was quite motivated. Smoked past 2 other guys and worked hard through the shoot. Left it all out there and when I wanted to go into cruise mode, I reached and banged the last few athletes. 35:53 5-mile finish. These distances are approximate and exaggerated a bit cause I "ain't" doing 7 minute miles, but still a gutsy performance for a "phat man!" 125:53 89/243 21/42 in one of THE toughest age categories with the top finishers all in this category. I've got much work to do and excited about possibly doing the mighty Montauk half ironman. I spoke to a guy about volunteering next weekend for free entry, which may be quite doable. He also mentioned programs for my kids, which I'm looking into for this winter.

FAST FOWARD TO OYSTER BAY & PT. LOOKOUT LOCAL TRI'S

39253 FROM: Fleet Subject: karen is my love! 184 Sunday, August 20, 2006 09:37 PM Host: ool-

Just popped by to see scoot's bday wishes (thanks buddy) and saw my darlin' wife's post! 'Twas a great day cranking a local tri and finishing 25/107 in age group and pouring brews from 10-12 after the race. My buddy brings the brews and gets me a free entry into race. I did the vip treatment for parking and had a great day! Nice race considering little to no training since Lp. Did a 56 bike yesterday and it was a sweet pre-race tune up! Love you guys! Point Lookout closes out the season once again. Details of the race are quite similar to '05 with a few exceptions. A little faster and stronger as the course is a true 3/4 mile swim with the town getting permits to go as far as Malibu beach. Swim was it's traditional vicious self with 250 people charging off the beach to get around one buoy. I got caught on the rope and one guy was climbing all over me and preventing me from escaping the nasty tide and the grip of the rope. A little shoulder push to boost my body away from him, the rope and the buoy and I was finally free. The guy came back at me as we both struggled to get into a rhythm. Finally, common sense and caution prevailed and we moved out of the death grip in this brutal ocean passageway. I was moving comfortably with absolutely no traffic, which pretty much told me I was off course and well behind despite my jump on the field. I later found out that you did not have to go around the start buoy and most of the field flew by. I suddenly found myself grabbing for dirt as I was washed ashore and forced to swim back out to get around the last buoy. I emerged from the water in 21 minutes, well behind the leaders and began my plight to picking off the field. I chopped away out of the saddle, jockeyed with a couple of guys and at mile 10 passed a huge pack of cyclists. In and out of transition at 54 minutes and it was time to chase down as many people as possible. Once again, I wait until the last mile at the turn- around, which is Malibu beach, and finish the job, gutting it out and leaving nothing on the course. Finishing time was around 1:24 on a longer course. I was 12/38 in age group to close the summer "festivus with the rest of us!" 62/242 picking off 6 dudes at the end, none in my age group, but a solid finish!

# 2008 Ironman Triathlon at Lake Placid: "Swan Song"

## Long Island Marathon '08

I'm not sure which is more painful, missing my established goal time of 3:30 and failing to qualify for the 2009 Boston Marathon or writing this race report. I'm certain it's obviously the ladder and actually not so bad to put my thoughts on paper to help learn some lessons and knock down that bad boy next time. I knew in the back of my mind that I neglected a few details in training and diet that was going to make this adventure much more difficult and somewhat unattainable. I took the simple approach of covering distance, speed and hill work in each workout, never separating out or plodding a course that works specifically on these crucial areas. I also lacked the discipline of managing my weight and had difficulty even in the last week of watching my calories. I made a feeble attempt at monitoring and managing my weight by writing down on a calendar my daily consumption, but that was tedious and didn't yield any great results. It was somewhat helpful because it forced me to take a good look and my diet/nutrition, giving me some tangible and concrete areas that I need to improve. I already know my weaknesses and it comes down to trying to put better limitations, not only for racing, but also for better quality of life and improved eating habits in general. I'm confident that as I move past this a moderate adjustment to both training and diet can certainly buy those few extra precious minutes and get me to the next level.

Despite falling short of my goal, a 3:40 is still a respectable time and was well earned over many months of training. A total of 9, 19 milers, 42, 13 milers, a truckload of sevens as well as swimming, biking and various miscellaneous categories of weight training and yard work about sums it up! A 10 month total of 2,820 miles/166 hours on the bike; 1,174 miles/170 hours running; 32 hours swimming; and 144 hours of miscellaneous training. A little more then 512 hours or 3 weeks of training! Part one of the racing season is complete and Ironman USA at Lake Placid is just around the corner. The base work is done and the next 2 months will get pretty intense with 6 centuries and 3 19 milers as a weekend warrior, combined with mid-week spinning, swimming and running. The total training summary will jump to new heights and the pressure will once again rear its ugly head!

The rehearsal and continued voicing of hours logged is the greatest weapon to managing stress and keeping that strong mental edge. What I lack physically is made-up in sheer, mental toughness. "Just another 13 miler", or "one more time around Central Park" is just a few examples of what takes me over the top. The race went off well, but there was a new intensity on this day that made this day extremely difficult. I wanted to quit a couple times and just go back to being a finisher. Doing a race is easy, racing a race is tough and you have to be very careful about knowing your limitations and being realistic about your ability and the work you've done to accomplish your goals. I felt like I was way in over my head at this race and pulled back a bit. I followed a plan to the letter that Aaron provided, checking splits and waiting for the 22-mile marker to let it all hang out. I did the math over and over and I was close to closing the deal. I needed 2, 7-minute miles at 24 and I dug deep! I was really disappointed when I hit the park with 1 mile to go and it was 3:25. I needed a 5-minute mile and despite the unrealistic possibility, I dug deeper and went for it with no reservations.

I stepped to the grass to soften the blows and BAM! My left calf went into spasms, my entire right leg followed suit and I did a nosedive into the grass to try to work it out! I squirmed and winced on the ground and attempted to relax and stop the madness. Suddenly, out of nowhere, my buddy Bob Cook, owner of Runners Edge and fellow Lake Placid ironman, swooped down to my rescue. He had a bottle of Gatorade, helped me to my feet and told me I can still get in with a descent time. It was quite miraculous and despite the fact that 25 people passed me in that last half mile, which bumped me to 105th place in the race, it was great to be able to be able to get to the finish.

You have to be smart and weigh your options and be aware of consequences when you step it up and go for it! I left it all out there like never before and there was no quit. I managed to get 23/66 in my age group, 105/454 and another major notch in mental and physical toughness that will carry me safely to Lake Placid.

My friend Caryn from Rye, who carried the torch with me in the 2000 Ironman parade, had a spectacular day finishing in 3:57, 1st in her age group and qualifying for Boston after missing the cut-off by 2 minutes in Philadelphia. My darling wife Karen, my angels Casey and Amy as always are my biggest inspiration as I continue to try to make them proud and be a good role model. As always, they awaited my finish and picked up the pieces, supporting me and cheering me up after a tough day.

A final brief story that will hopefully serve as a convincing reminder of what's important in life is an anecdote from race morning. I sat in the bathroom making final preparations and fiddling with my wedding ring. It slipped off my finger, bounced and rolled on the floor. It was slow-motion footage as my precious, etched with infinite symbols, fine golden ring slid under the radiator and down the crack between the tiles. My wife came to my rescue and somehow managed to get hold of it and return it safely to my finger. I don't know if its irony or coincidence, maybe one day I'll figure out the difference, but this much I know. The training that I meticulously, methodically, and carefully plan with unyielding will and desire must be transferred some way back to the family. We get so caught up in ourselves, the training, and the races, that we forget what is most important. Hopefully, as I plunge deeper into the spring, I will not forget the little race morning reminder that ended well and put a smile on my face.

## The Yorktown Ride

The evening of the first ride in the mountains is upon me and the pressure is building from the anticipation of an uncharted flight. I'm familiar with the massive terrain that is Bear Mountain and the subtle, yet definite reality that as you pass through Nyack and get a taste for some hills, Perkins road and the trip home will soon be at a screaming all time high in pain and determination. This trip, however, has many uncertainties, which includes the 70-mile drive to the starting location and the new path that we will chisel out for the day.

Brian Carver, the leader of multiple excursions in the past, will have a new name at the conclusion of this day and will be better known as Brian "Carve-him" a new one. Oh yes, one thing is certain! We will see the great Bear and Perkins road and multiply that by ten, putting together one of the most difficult days in the saddle ever known! It's a day were the ipod is left at home to make certain I can see the sights and hear the sounds of the day. It's a day that I now know that I have to train better just to prepare for a training day. I've always said that as we prepare for ironman, you need days that you are sleep deprived based on fear for what you are about to experience. I now know that utter peril awaits me in three weeks when I attempt to tackle this route again!

We climbed out of Brian's neighborhood and very quickly found ourselves on the smoothest, cleanest, car-free bike path imaginable. It was cold from the overcast of trees, but relaxing in terms of safety and nice to finally be on our way. We exited the cart path, headed back in a similar direction parallel with the path and began to climb on long winding roads. We approached Peekskill and eased through the town, enjoying the historical sights.

We found ourselves at the first fueling station, which would be our last for the next 50 miles, with the exception of some vending machines. I mentioned that I could not figure out how to get my speedometer to the setting that stops when you are no longer riding, thus affecting your final estimated output. When I came out of the shop, it was all set with just the press of a button. Four years went by with the process of turning on and off, sometimes forgetting and just like that I was on autopilot. Sometimes the simplest solutions are sitting right in front of us and we have no clue! Luckily, Brian had a clue and hooked me up. "Anywho", surely I digress. It was the beginning of visiting with an old friend that I did not admire in the least. It was a climb across the Bear Mountain Bridge that in my first experience was an unexpected downhill nightmare that taught me many lessons about going aero in the mountains and knowing my limitations. This, however was uphill, but a gentle reminder of the nasty drops that we would encounter throughout the day.

I say nasty as I'd much prefer the painful, arduous task of climbing then the paralyzing, handlebar gripping, Zipp tossing, hang on to your life type descents that leave you screaming and crying for your mommy! It was soon after that we had arrived at Bear Mountain and began the 3-mile trip to the peak. It seems to get steeper every year and as my buddy shoots off to the top, I'm humbled by the countless number of Northern veterans skating past me.

I arrive at the top and the breeze is giving me a chill as we chat with members of a Manhattan based bike club on a reunion tour. A couple of people are from Riverdale School where Brian is the swim coach and now the Dean of students. I prompt him to get moving as we are only at mile 25 and I'm getting chilled to the bone. We head out to Harriman state park and while the hills continue to hinder any kind of descent speed work, the climbing in invaluable for Lake Placid.

We arrive at the loop and encounter the Genesis Adventure Series sponsoring a quarter and half-ironman race. We are traveling in the opposite direction, which is fine until we reach the 1500-mile elevation and getting bombarded with tri-freaks whaling down the steep embankment. We manage our space, suck up the 16-mile loop and somehow survive one of the biggest slopes since Keene that clocked Brian in at 50 M.P.H.! I stayed within my limits, nearly got tossed a few times with the wind ripping through my 81mm rims and kept it at a conservative 38 m.p.h.

We exited the park and went back to the palisades parkway that brought us back to Bear Mountain. The sign read "Perkins Road Next Exit"! I couldn't believe we were heading back up the mountain! We climbed out of our saddles again as it was impossible to sit without falling over. We managed to get through this section and coasted down to the picnic grounds. At this point we stopped to refuel at the vending machines and I begged and pleaded to find a path home that was somewhat reasonable. It was not to be.

We headed out of the park and cruised for 10 miles with a stiff wind in our face, but still moving at a pretty good clip. It was nice to finally get something going, but that little joy ride was just about over. We fueled up and the attendant in the shop asked which way we were going. We told him we were heading to Yorktown and his eyes rolled to the back of his head as he exclaimed and pointed, "you're going that way?" He thought we were pretty crazy and we told him if he had only known where we had already been, he would be certain of that fact. And so off we went and as the climbing began another rider approached and confirmed the fact that we were in for another 20 nasty, uphill miles. "Strap in boys, 'cause you're about to get crushed!"

He wasn't kidding as we hit another 4-5 "out-of-the-saddle type hills and quietly, calmly tried to keep it all together. Finally, we started skating on some of the most beautifully traveled roads and closed the gap on the distance. Despite some re-assurance by a much tamer, landscape, the damage was done and there were still no guarantees that the pain train had left the station. The sign for Yorktown was big and bold and it looked like we were going to make it! But not before we had to walk the bikes over a small fence and hike it up one more incline. The day was done and although I bagged the brick, which has become a traditional follow-up, I had all I could handle and still an uncertain drive back to Long Island. A monumental day in the saddle, more lessons learned and a step closer to the finish line.

## Yorktown Ride/Revisited

It has always been said that to train for ironman, one must find days that can best emulate race day and as such, bring out emotions that stir the mind, body and soul leading up to the day. The nervous rambling, the strange eating patterns and the sleepless nights are just a few indications that the weekend is looking mighty brutal. This trip had an additional edge to it, because the amount of climbing, now combined with 95-degree temperatures was no longer a mystery. We cut through this path before, and while at least the aspect of uncertainty in the terrain was lessoned by our experience, there are always question marks that remain. Will the 60 mile commute go as planned, how will the heat affect our performance, is the wind going to play a role today, can we make it up that last hill without blowing up? The questions and uncertainties are endless which I guess is why it makes these days so interesting.

The evening before the ride is always difficult as the pressure mounts and I fail to offer anything to my family as I become unraveled with all my worries, fears, and question marks, not just on the day, but on our life and our future. Our family has been through some difficult times this year, but this month has been the all time test and moving forward, managing life, staying focused and making the correct choices and decisions has reached all time heights. Making the decision to even head to the mountains posed yet another conflict in my mind, and while my lovely wife Karen supports my plans and decisions, she also has to deal with my idiosyncratic behavior prior to each of these days which seem to be more frequent then in previous years as I extend the training platform.

The alarm was set for 4 a.m. and I was on the move. The morning is a good place for me as I enjoy finally being in the moment and getting busy doing what I spent the entire week worrying about and obsessing. I already felt good about the commute as I worked out some of the kinks, making the trip more predictable, allowing me to focus on other things. I did not anticipate the "pea soup" fog that prevented me from seeing the exit signs, but luckily felt confident about the directions, despite my navigationally challenged disposition, and forged on to Yorktown. Upon my arrival, I saw 2 deer prancing across the road and knew I was in a good place. Brian was ripped and ready to go and it was only 6 a.m., light fog and the mood was outstanding. We were pedaling by 630 a.m. and despite the impending heat on the day, we were able to get to the top of Bear Mountain, 30 miles of our trip accomplished before the sun reared it's blistering heat.

We were up in the mountains, riding past rivers, streams and had plenty of shade to keep us cool. The air was still as glass and I can't remember any trip in which going "aero" felt so safe and taking every down hill for all that it was worth was even in the realm of possibility. I had land marked a couple of twisting, hairy downhill's in traffic and had already managed a strategy for navigating these portions safely. Harriman state park was pure joy and despite the over 1500 feet of drops and elevations, the park was all ours on the day! Bear Mountain yielded a 15-minute improvement over the last trip and with 40 miles to go we were feeling good. We managed the next 5-mile stretch and agreed that the wind at our back was truly our friend, unlike our first trip. We made the turn a little sooner to avoid some of the nastier, uncovered, step roadways as the heat index rose to above 100!

We still had to deal with many steep climbs and while the length was shortened, there were some way over the top ridges that came dangerously close to stopping us dead in out tracks and keeling over. We doubled back to a flat section that we started out day that was slightly shaded, but Brian had come apart from the heat and was hobbling home. I did some speed work on the path and then we made a pit stop to get my buddy up and moving for the last 12 miles. It was a steady ride along the road at a nice pace, but then there is the final climb into Yorktown. We came upon a section that narrowed, crossed over an intersection and Brian gave me a shout, "U-Haul trailer at your back!" There was about a foot that separated this busty trailer and me and with 4 miles to go, one of those questionable uncertainties was answered with a positive result.

We arrive home and cut 20 minutes off our previous attempt. It was a scorching 95 degrees which was 30 degrees greater then when we departed at 630 a.m. A quick change as I am working hard on transition and out for a 4 mile run in a park that was not supposed to have any hills nearly as steep as central park. That was false, but I put on my Lake Placid glasses that show me short clips of those finishing hills at tore that sucker down! Brian pedaled along side with drinks and moral support. He would be racing at Harriman a local tri in an attempt to retain his 1st place title from last year. We worked through the heat and finished with 4 miles at 8:30 and one step closer to getting it done.

## Ride to Montauk

The ride to Montauk holds a special place in the history of cycling that goes back to 1999. In my debut of triathlons and consequently the beginning of race reports, I mentioned my best friend, Peter Cotter that has been there from the start and creating a landscape in his life's' pursuit that can only be compared to a Picasso canvas, or more specifically, a work of art! I dedicate and honor this ride report to Pete, who sponsored this glorious spin to the east end of Long Island and makes me proud to call him my brother! Over the past 20 years, most of my travels and adventures, with the exceptions of my lovely wife Karen, have been with Pete. We talked about those adventures this past weekend, which included our backpacking trip when we first met, countless concert tours in which we traveled to Maryland, Pennsylvania, Virginia, Florida and a magnificent trip to Hawaii. We were not involved in ironman at the time, but in a recent visit back to the islands, Pete spoke to Cowman, who was one of the original cast of characters that started this wacky sport. The point I'm trying to make is that after all these years of traveling around, searching for a future, we have found ourselves gathering at different events which includes one of the most popular triathlons on long island at Oyster Bay, and most recently the ride to Montauk. We toast and cheer with the finest Brew in the world, that which is Bluepoint, and it blows my mind when I think about the fact that Pete Cotter is leading the charge!

The ride itself had some twists and turns, both figuratively and literally. In all my years, I have never taken a ride past exit 62 on the service road. It has always been 33 miles to Cotters' house and whatever I can find in between. I ventured past this spot on one occasion last summer, checking out my old stomping grounds as a youth and it was a disaster. I found myself on narrow shoulders and traffic moving at 75 M.P.H.! I crawled back to Cotters' and called it a day. You can only imagine my concerns as I viewed the travel sheet and there were hundreds of turns to get to Montauk! I thought it would be one straight road all the way east, but that was not to be! I hooked up with a guy who got me to the first rest stop. I was less then patient in pushing the pace as the guilt for riding a flat course instead of attending my daughter's soccer tournament began to weigh in heavy on my mind. I knew that since I was not to be denied this classic Cotter ride, I needed to at least get in a solid day of training. My speedometer did not work properly and so the first leg of this tour was an estimate. I began the second stretch on my own and followed the markings that were fantastically placed on the roads. It was difficult to lay your head down and grind it out, while still trying to find the markers. Eventually I developed a confidence and started cranking it out. I rode past beautiful farms, houses and beach resorts that I frequented many moons ago. I slid in and out of the next rest stop, refusing to take any kind of a break.

It was heating up and I cranked it all the way to the Hamptons. Many of us were at a standstill as the markers were paved over and directions became challenging. I hooked up with a guy named John, who called his sister at the Green Thumb, which was the final rest stop and she walked us in. John and I put the hammer down for the final 30 miles and when we arrived in Montauk, there was the one hill to climb, the only one on the day and we were both feeling it! I could feel my legs cramping and could not believe this course could have that affect. A combination of continuous riding with almost no stopping with the few rest stops and an all out assault on the course yielded an unprecedented day in the saddle. 104 miles in 5:30ish and one for the books. Despite my late start, there were only a handful of hard-core riders at the finish. It would be hours before Cotter and the rest of the crew would arrive. Marcus, Keith, Dianne, and Vince completed 80 miles and for some it more then doubled their longest ride. Many proud faces arrived at different times, all with goals, dreams and milestones reached. The brews poured for over 8 hours as some people finished as late as 8 p.m. I went back to the Montauk Manor and eventually met up with Jen, Pete's lovely bride and some friends in town for dinner. We returned to the Manor and Pete and I walked the grounds under "Northern Lights", remembering those lost souls that fought and died for this great land. And as the sun set on one of the longest days of the year, one of the main themes that resonated on this historical site and must always be remembered was described by James Morrison, a famous poet..."Indians scattered on dawns highway, bleeding, ghosts crowd the young childs' fragile egg-shelled mind!"

## The Closer

It was not the first trip to Bear Mountain and it certainly was not the first 100 miler, but it was the first solo century to Bear Mountain and a trip I had not taken since back in 2006. Previously this season my training in the mountains was staged from Yorktown with my good friend Brian, but he would be in Lake Placid this weekend and therefore I was flying on my own with clipped wings based on my challenged navigational skills. In addition, the return trip home when we previously did the ride from Manhattan was via Englewood cliffs, which cut off the area of 9w that I now recall as being clutch for managing a more safe and efficient ride. I came real close to bailing on this ride on the evening before setting the alarm for 4:30 a.m., upon arriving in Manhattan the next day and about 5 miles out in which I was already lost! I forgot my bag initially which had my wallet and keys, but luckily noticed this and immediately retrieved it from home. I forgot my gloves and tried to convince myself that based on the humid conditions it's best until my hands were slipping and the argument was lost. I pushed those thoughts out of my mind, sucked it up and began my trip. I was quite shaky to start based on these factors and reminded myself to stay calm, pay careful attention to the roads, manage the directions to the George Washington Bridge and then build upon that success. Immediately, I sensed that I was off course and got directions from an early morning walker. She sent me in the right direction and when I spotted a guy riding, I followed him and inquired about the bridge. He gave me the guided tour and the first step was safely accomplished.

I worked through the hairpin turns of the ramp leading across the bridge, the "box-trot" as I like to call it around the trestles and shot out the other side. I began to feel comfortable and at peace with the directions. However, so much of my energy was drained from a sleepless night, uncertainties, little mistakes in equipment, and navigation that I began to worry if I had enough strength to get through this final trip! The temperature was quickly rising, I was late getting out and what I thought to have been my most difficult ride over a month ago suddenly seemed like it would rate as a much easier day in the saddle then that which I was about to experience. I stayed in my zone, drank plenty of fluids and continued to whisk away the miles. The territory was pretty familiar as I've done this trip over a dozen times in one form or another, but still, this was the closer! I land marked certain spots and placed a mental image in my mind for the return trip. It was impossible to count how many hills there were, so I noted as many of the big ones and continued to focus. I passed Nyack, Haverstraw, and reached Stony Point, re-fueling for the last time before the big push to the peak. I cruised past the final rock wall that has always been a brutal spot on this ride, but forgot how very long and steep from the entrance of the park, to Perkins road and the last "stair-stepper" of a climb that I was about to encounter. I made it to the top and had no intention on sticking around for the view, as I was anxious to get this thing over! I found a shady spot, a quick drink, some crackers and zipped up for the long slide back down the mountain. I rolled with it, cooled off, stretched and prepped for the carnage that would be my thrashed body after the next 50 miles. Originally on this ride I thought that heading south meant down hill all the way home. "Johnny woops, Johnny woops and wee, wee, wee, wee, all the way home" This was no nursery rhythm and it was time to man up and strap in!

I knew the hills would be brutal and continued to stay in a reasonable zone. I also knew that the nasty, narrow, non-shoulder pathway in which I was about to travel would soon be a harsh reality and tried to stay focused. I got caught up in a crew traveling back to the city and despite my navigational fears; I chose solo over caravan, as that is just not my style. Once again, I fueled up and prepared for the final climbs back to the bridge. Rockland county state park marks one of the bigger climbs around the 80- mile mark and for the record, one other state park for future reference. I saw the signs for Englewood, the palisades parkway and started to think I went too far and missed a turn. A little further up the road I determined that I was on course and then saw the bridge, that beautiful George Washington Bridge. There was a line of traffic across the span and I patiently got in line with all the other bikers and put on my "safety helmet". We managed the path and then I gave it my best to hammer it home to make up for some lost pacing on the bridge. Unfortunately, my speedometer was shot from the start and so my estimate is based on real time that had me departing at 6:50 a.m. and back at 1:40 p.m. Based on quick stops in 4-5 locations I figure around 6:20 finishing time on the day. I quickly dropped my bike at the gym, filled my water bottles and headed out for a 7-mile loop of central park. It was packed with joggers, cyclists, sunbathers, strollers, guitar heroes and I felt like waving the American flag in this parade like atmosphere. Despite the heat, I was excited to be wrapping up what has amounted to a year long training regiment and somewhat bitter sweet, as I was taking my last loop of the park until September. My pace was outstanding, but at the bottom of the museum mile, my core body temp spiked and it was time to water down or face serious consequences. I covered myself in cool water and refilled my bottles for the last uphill mile. A reasonable 64-minute, 7 miler and the deal was done! Ready or not, here I come!

# Swan Song

"It is the springtime of my loving, the second season, I'm to know; You are the sunlight in my growing, so little warmth, I've felt before; Speak to me only with your eyes, it is to you I bring this tune..." This was my 5th ironman triathlon at Lake Placid in it's 10th anniversary and like all the one's in the past, it is a long, arduous trip the start line in which there are no guarantees. The over 4000 miles of bike training, 1400 miles running, 40 hours of swimming, 52 hours of weight and miscellaneous training is complete and all that remains is in the hands of God. At the risk of sounding cliché, the only thing you can control on race week is your attitude, which has the greatest impact on the final result.

Race week brings with it incredible stress as we are challenged to keep ourselves in check with limited training. We have to avoid overstuffing our neurotic pie-wholes and slicing our fingers off with the electric saw as we do small projects around the house to keep our sanity. More specifically in my case is dealing with the social aspects of hosting a family from Oregon, which included many dinners out and on the road, as well as a barbeque that was a little too much for a Monday prior to the race. It was a good distraction for the most part and considering the potential for collateral damage it went well. I still had 2 full days to pack and prepare for our 4 am departure and slide into position for the race.

We began our trip and as we arrived on the ramp to the Meadowbrook Parkway, we noticed the road was completely closed to construction. We, however, merged on the road just past the closure and were happily on our way with our first drop of good karma. Oh, did I just say, "drop of good Karma?" We can talk more, much more about that later! We managed the trip in less than 5 hours, arriving in Lake Placid by 9:30 am and went into registration mode. Karen takes Casey and Amy to the pool and like clockwork we follow the plan that has worked for years. I arrive at registration and at the back of the line is my training buddy Brian from Yorktown Heights that I took many trips to Bear Mountain. It's great to chat with him about our final preparations as he did some racing and training in lake Placid and I closed it out with a Montauk ride and a classic solo trip from Manhattan which poetically concludes with a 7 mile run of central park.

It's that strange magic that can not be explained as I head back to meet with the family and we gear up for the kids splash and dash race. The kids decide that they are not going to do the race and as we relax in the hotel, the skies open up and it's thunder, lightning, a total downpour and yet, another bullet is dodged. The sky clears and I decide it's time to take my traditional loop around the lake. I gear up, head down and depart from the hotel beach in the direction of the swim start. The water is comfortable, but my wet suit is tight and my left leg beneath my knee is getting chaffed. I get to the beach and there's a guy just standing in the water that I nearly bump into as I make my final approach. I stand up and he apologizes. I look back and its "Slowpoke" AKA "Bernie the attorney", one of my best friends from Long Island competing in his 2nd ironman. I'm starting to think this is just plain weird and overly coincidental that within a few hours of being in Lake Placid I've accidentally and literally have bumped into my two main men! We chat for a while and I get back to swimming the loop.

I get half way around the lake and begin to have a mild panic attack in the water! It just so happens that I have a propensity to calf pulls when swimming that renders me completely incompetent in the water. More times then I care to admit I have found myself grabbing for ropes in the pool, with the latest episode on the last swim of the last lap in the town pool. It's no secret that the swim is a deal breaker for me in this race and despite my 20 years of lifeguard experience and close to 10 years of racing, you can begin to understand the title of my report. I decide to make a "bee" line for the hotel, which is directly to my left, but much further off the line then anticipated. In reality, the distance from line to shore makes up the difference in distance, which remained to the last buoy, so at least I maintained a portion of a psychological edge. I arrived at the hotel and was hooked by some kids fishing off the dock. "We got a big one", they shouted! I couldn't agree more, a big fish out of water am I!

I was still feeling good, despite my horrific fears of the swim that continued to mount and break me down. I pushed it aside and remained focused. It was time to meet up with my family and my brother Tony, his wife Lynn, and my 6' 4" 225 pound 19-year-old nephew that made the trip for the second time in the past two years at Lake Placid. Unfortunately, they had transportation woes coming all the way from Florida and so my girls and I went for dinner and then it was off to IBSEX. We were the first to arrive with the exception of Mary and her husband, who would later be best known as a popular character from Marvel comics and was a huge hit throughout the day. A gal named Jo was there, not Oreo jo who we missed along with Kelly, Schack, Sto, Hammy, Cindee, Kinger, Latrick, Coach Jean HHH, BBB, DTK, BOFF and so many others, but apparently an inaugural jo, which she made pretty clear throughout the night. Josef, who I later found out was not Spanish, (but then again neither am I, despite the name Armata aka Fleet) was in attendance with his wife.

My brother and his family arrived and it was a great reunion. Tony is a sweetheart and one of my best friends! Big Fella, Scoot, Dug, Garv and Banger arrived which meant Garvaid would be in full swing and that kind of support/abuse on the run course 4 times is enough to get you pumped and keep the good times a rollin'! Schep arrived triumphantly after a 200 mile solo bike effort to Lake Placid along with uncle Terry that was still wondering, "why did I let Wicked Wanda sign me up again?" Bernie the attorney, aka slowpoke was wondering the same thing, but among many had the opportunity to personally thank Wanda, who might have not made the trip without the help of Chip her husband and her daughter Chelsea. Traci arrived with her children and her mom and was ready to go! Burke showed up with his wife and Weston who has been doing a documentary of ironman also made an appearance. Finally, the Mayor Woodman graced us with his presence in his unprecedented 10 out of 10 trips to Lake Placid, which included one year all the way from Vietnam and competing in his 19th ironman. He is truly the Mayor of our friendly forum and an inspiration to all of us. I was sad that Nanook did not make it and we never had a chance to see each other, but I know he was with us all weekend and had a great race. Caryn from Rye also missed our grand affair, but we caught up with her later that weekend. Local clubs like Team in Training with head coach Steve Tarpinian whose colors I fly in the race as well as Bob Cook, Jose Lopez, Barbara Cronnin-Stagnari, Meredith DeRossa, Rich Barkin from Runners Edge were in town for the race either supporting or competing. I also ran into former training partners Carmello and Daryn that I met at the aqua center and was excited to see in town. The players were all in the house and it was time to get one final good night sleep, as race day evening is pretty much a bust in terms of solid sleep.

The post-race day includes final preparations, test ride taken on the run course, which includes a visit with the cherries and bears in the final hill of the bike course, and packing up for the big bike sleepover. I ride conservatively down the hill and out of town. At the bottom of the hill my front tire explodes and similar to 2006, I have gotten a flat on my test ride and knocked them out of my system. The good karma continues to flow and I'm really feeling like I'm being helped dramatically to the start line. It seems the biggest bump in the road has only come from my own paranoid, delusional breakdown in the water, thus reconfirming our old cliché; it's your attitude!

I return to the hotel just in time for the rain to start pouring down and my grin is uncontrollable and yet another strange confirmation in fate and the path I'm following is being cleared. I pack my bags, swing down to the oval and kiss Jenny II goodnight. "We are going to have a great ride tomorrow!" I called Bernie and we began to review some questions he had regarding final preparations. I was trying to be patient, but the oval was a little over an hour before being closed and Bernie has nothing ready! We climb the monster hill to the Crowne Plaza and begin sorting through his stuff. I'm mortified by his choice of costume, er, ah race clothes, but excited about the fact that he finally learned how to clip into his Bike. Bernie is me back in 2000, with little training, experience, a heart of gold and a long, long day ahead of him. His lovely wife Jen is wheeling around 3 young children, which is one more then my brave, caring, and courageous wife had when we were in this situation 9 years ago.

His sticker sheet with his numbers were printed backwards and when they reprinted them incorrectly a sweet, buffed women that only came up to his chest offered some words of encouragement. Heather told Bernie not to sweat the small stuff and to make the numbers work. He was fine with that and would later learn that he received advice from the queen of Lake Placid herself...that's right...Heather Fuhr! It just does not get any better then that as we close out final preparations and prepare for the ironman!

Race morning arrives and in many ways it's a combination of relief and total terror. So many fantastic details of race day preparation are behind us, but the cold, darkness of the mountains prior to the race and the tension in the air is indescribable and it takes every part of your positive being to release the paralyzing affects of the morning and get ready to tow the line. You rehearse in your head all you've done and one by one you begin to see friends that relieve the tension. I see Caryn for the first time and I am relieved that she made it to the start. Mary and her marvel-comic dressed husband are creating a stir and putting smiles on people's faces. Special needs bags are dropped, bike is checked and that last porta-potty visit is nerve racking as they announce the close of the transition area and prompt people to get to the start. I'm still not body marked and trying to stay calm.

Finally I get my turn and go to get marked. Age 44 marked on one calf and a smiley face on the other to help spread the cheer. The march to the swim and it feels like I'm going to the gallows. I see Brian's wife Melissa and she greets me with a smile and sends me on my way with wonderful words of encouragement. I'm feeling parched and a community Gatorade is passed. I get in the water and establish my position by the dock. I'm feeling dehydrated and already starting to panic that my calf may blow if I'm already in this state. I spot a bottle on the dock and that wonderful feeling of being watched and taken care of returns with a rush. A woman turns to me and says "That official just saw you drink from the bottle and may dq you for abandoning equipment." I began to argue with her, explaining that it's not my bottle and then decided I'm wasting good energy, downed the remainder of the water and slid away. Some of that positive energy was lost on that exchange, but then the "Star-Spangled Banner" began and standing directly next to me with his hand on his heart is non other than Mayor Woody Freese! I needed nothing else to send me off with the absolute greatest amount of confidence. I then spotted Caryn and paid it forward as she exclaimed what great vibes from that brief meeting was quite helpful in starting her day!

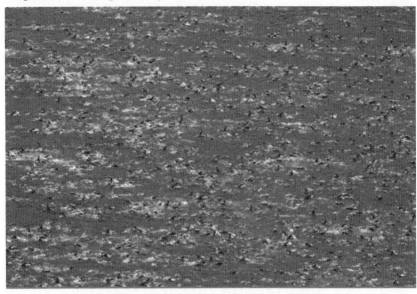

The cannon exploded and the maniacs were slapping, kicking, thrashing while I held my ground. I followed my plan, slid along the dock and worked my way to the left. I began to swim on my own terms next to the support team and followed the boat line as opposed to the one with three thousand maniacs. I was feeling exhausted, anxious, and began to panic. The race was going on without me to the right and I was doing all the work without the benefit of the draft. You can't have it both ways, either solo and safe or psycho and draft. I finally made the move and compromised a bit to get back in the race. I wanted to quit, but there's just no turning around after going so far to the start. I lowered my head, cranked to the end, made the turn and found the line. It was all good and I finally knew I was through the hardest part of the swim. I climbed out of the first loop and the pro time was 50 minutes, which put me at 40 minutes. I did the math wrong and thought I was on pace for a 1:30 which had not been done since 2000. I jumped back in, found the line and owned it the rest of the swim. It was miraculous! Nobody was near me? I couldn't figure it out and with the exception of one breast "stroker", whom I finally zipped around, I had the entire lake to myself? The rain started pouring down, but I could care less as this deal breaker was just about broken and I was on my way with a 1:18 finish! A few minutes more then last time, but given my paralyzing, overly conservative, off the line approach from the start, I was thrilled. Stripped off the suit and greeted my family braving the beginning of a long day in the rain as I jogged carefully on a slippery mat to the oval.

Melissa gives me the thumbs up and sends me down the ramp. Her husband Brian banged a: 59 and it was nice to see her sticking around another 20 minutes for us late arrivals. The change tent was foggy, smelly, dirty and totally packed. Plenty of motivation to get up and out, while making sure, to have all the necessities in 12 minutes. The vest was a "no brainer" and I almost did not pack it! It saved the day, as it's no secret the remainder of this race would be about the rain that not only did not stop; it pelted us sideways and took its best shot at crippling the field. A constant theme, which is obvious and repeated frequently in my mind was, "I'm out of the water and nothing can stop me now!" The first loop had its challenges, which includes keeping the rubber side down on Keene with a continuous, deliberate and carefully calculated break job throughout this nasty slope of terror!

The force-feeding in the rain began and trying to stay warm continued to be an issue. The energy was being sucked from your body as you attempted to hang on to your bike from crashing and curl your body in close in an effort to stay warm. I heard somewhere that people urinate while riding and I could never quite understand this concept or imagine how this could be done? And so on this day, a new lesson was learned that was not only practical in terms of time conservation, but also outstanding as a tool to stay warm. The downhill's now served a "tri-fecta" which allowed you to rest, pee, and get warm all at the same time. Please understand while this may seem to some as disgusting, it was practical and necessary. Imagine your bodily functions are actually aiding you in surviving what was a continuous on slaughter of rain, hail, and some of the nastiest conditions I have ever faced! There were times I had to tip my helmet down to prevent the blinding rain from punishing me any further.

The first loop was over in 3:10 and I wa happy after seeing my family in our traditional 56-mile marker to climb out of town, fist pumping the crowd and brave one more loop. I kept repeating the theme, "I'm out of the water", but the cynical side of me was getting sick and tired of that mantra as we were seemingly never getting out of the water.

It was time to conquer Keene again and what has always been repeated is "don't let this slippery slope end your day!" Managed to sail through this section, but not without a price. The cold, hard, rain combined with monster nervous tension left me with spasms in my back and more and more tightness in my legs that should otherwise be the case at mile 66. I eased into the next section, knowing that I had to find some recovery before the final stretch of grueling ups that is inherent in this course for close to the last 30 miles. I continued to eat like a champ and began to mentally prepare for the marathon. There were some signs of a break in the rain only to come back with a more furious dousing that became laughable. I was fine as I approached town and laid my final bit of rubber on the pavement with a 3:25 second loop and a 6:35ish finish.

I was greeted by my family, Peter Cotter, his lovely wife Jen and little Sophie who smiled and fist pumped me from the hill. A beautiful magical site along with my gorgeous wife, daughters and family as I went to lace up my shoes for the beast!

The run is a good place for me, out of transition in 8 minutes and my goal of 12:29 is in reach. I depart from the tent and search for my children. Despite some warnings about spectators being too close, I swing next to the barrier, grab my Casey and Amy smooches and head down the hill. The pounding is ridiculous and you can't feel your legs. "At least it's not raining" was a mistake as it began to pour once again. "At least I'm out of the water?" I giggled and moved on to find Garv-aid in tact. The Fuller brothers, Schep, Big Fella, Garv, Art, and to my surprise, the return of Johno, who has been missing in action from the page for over a year. The support is fantastic, but now the business of finding my legs and a bathroom is my biggest priority. I have a "no walk" policy on this course, but I probably overdo the bathroom stops, which pretty much include every other mile on the course. It's my way of taking a break, checking my heart rate and then getting back to the race. It works well for me and becomes necessary on this day as the cold, wet; rainy day has taken more from me then expected.

I reach the first timing mat at the end of the road and that's a huge lift as it's time to get back to town. I finish first loop in 2:15 and I'm afraid to let my family see me, as I'm a total train wreck! Mentally, I have no problem finishing this thing, but physically, I feel beat down and know that I have to be smart. I take one more bathroom stop, juiced up before seeing my family. I look fresh which is a combination of my rest stop method and acting job. Based on my condition, I re-establish my goals to play it safe and shoot for the sub 13-hour finish. It's not worth the medical tent, or potential hospital visit and possibly crashing completely. I stay with the plan, continue to shuffle and take my breaks while doing the math. I'm 9 miles away, reach for my endurolytes, which strangely enough I was no longer hearing in my fuel bag and they are gone! I have a momentary lapse and convince myself that between the drinks on the course, the fluids that I had been taking in like a champ, that I should be just fine. I didn't really believe it and given my history in the last marathon with a half mile to go that put me down with uncontrollable spasms, I had a hard time with this set back. Although Bob Cook, owner of runners edge and good friend was out supporting me on the course, he was not going to appear like an angel with a bottle of Gatorade in hand to save the day like he did at the Long Island Marathon.

I reminded myself that at the time I was trying to knock down a 5 minute mile to qualify for Boston, was in an all out sprint and abused myself in that last mile. I reminded myself to keep it real and stick with the plan. I was about to skip the next bathroom stop and once again, the voice inside my head said, "stick with the plan." I did just that and found a capsule with 7 endurolytes the exact amount needed for the last 90 minutes and I was totally stoked!

It was a pure pleasure ride from this point despite all the pain. I'm a moron, it's an oxymoron, irony, coincidence, never really get that, but who cares I'm going home! I know at this point it's been so much about survival on one of the most brutal days Lake Placid has ever dished out in it's 10 years and just getting it done in tact is totally medal! A final scream to garv-aid, the long haul up the hill and the smile returns to the face. I know that many folks still have another loop and a possible 3-4 more hours to go and my heart bleeds for them. I do my final thing down the home stretch and Wonderful Wanda is there to greet as she is always there and been tremendous over the years as a great support for this race. The finish had some anticipated challenges. My daughters have crossed the line every year and this year NA established a new rule that only allowed one child. I expressed my concerns to one of the top dogs and while he gave me the green light, the captain at the staging area threatened to dq me if I tried to bring both daughters through the line. My children are the true champs in voice and spirit as the unselfishly pleaded with me to continue through the shoot and not put my race in jeopardy. They get those virtues from their mother, my darling wife Karen, who has taken me to my 5th ironman finish with a 13:17 in it's 10th year anniversary!

It was time to clean up and get back to the oval for the midnight hour. Bernie was still out there amongst others like Burke who eventually finished at 17 hours and a few seconds and was given all the hardware. Way to go Burke! They were going to need some help coming home. We waited in anticipation for the final finishers and at 11:40 p.m. I saw Bernie with the green glow on his head that he wore like a crown. He's a king, a great friend and I was so happy to see him reach the line. We packed him up, wheeled his family up that nasty hill to the Plaza and then returned to gather all his belongings. It was a nostalgic finish to a time in 2000 when my wife's h.s buddy Kerry Fredericks, who lives in Saranac, was there to help me with my gear and family at midnight in one of the longest days of my life. It felt real good to be there for Bernie and somehow pay it forward.

We closed the trip on Tuesday with a 17 mile, 6 hour, class III-IV whitewater rafting trip that pretty much took me out! No report for this one, but in short, I was scared to death, mostly for my children and my body was really shot! I wound up slightly hypothermic, puked my guts out for the entire evening, spiked a nasty temperature and thought I was going to die! The reality was that despite how bad I felt, the rain that poured for 12 straight hours on the day of the ironman raised the water level on the river to a level that took us above the rocks and helped us to cruise safely home. The final day on the river could've put me away if it had not been for all that rain and what seemed to be all wrong on race day, was just right for my family on the river. The good karma that was with me throughout the trip never left my side. Despite appearances that masked itself in the form of torrential downpours, there was a reason, which is never really understood. The path that was paved to get to the finish was clearly a blessing and one in which I will forever be grateful!

# 2010 Ironman Triathlon at Lake Placid: "Unedited and Uniterupted

# Introduction '10

The final chapters are the most difficult to write. I have lyrics ringing in my head and this is usually a good starting point for me, but lessons learned on cost management of finishing my story prevent me from going in that direction. And yet I digress, and in hopes to jump-start and illustrate my closing chapters I remember what my old friend Jim once said, "Did you have a good world when you died, enough to base a movie on?" This line is a keeper and expresses deeply my concerns as I attempt to close out my thoughts and ultimately release my book. I become cynical and continue to brow beat myself for writing a story that barely qualifies for the "Funny Papers". No qualifying times to speak of at the Long Island Marathon for Boston in April, not even close to the 10:15 ironman finishing time to qualify for the World Championship in Kona and despite my unprecedented four trips to Bear Mountain, I can't even tell the story in which I squared off with a bear, much less a deer or even a chipmunk! Truth be told, I saw some wild life, but unfortunately most of it was in the way of road kill! I ask myself or should I say remind myself of what this has all been about, the goals established and the reasons for being involved in this sport and that helps to ease back in, re-focus, and find those precious final words.

The Long Island Marathon and subsequent trips to Bear Mountain, as well as the Ride to Montauk are months behind me and unlike in the past, I have absolutely none, nada, zilch in writing to fall back on to relive the experience. A time when I used to fire off a report to friends immediately following any race or tough training day has fallen at the waist side. The stage is set for a partially senile, slightly cynical, middle aged crisis of a man to reflect back and draw strength from and recall possible lessons learned in the rear and side view mirrors of his life. Anyone that drives knows that "objects in mirror are closer than they appear", but as I reflect back that little verbiage feels very far away from the truth.

## Long Island Marathon '10

It was hot, Africa hot on a spring day! That detail is easy to remember and is almost as vivid as the previous years' cold, rainstorm which followed my 2008 ironman that was over 13 hours in the pouring, frigid, hailstorm rain that closed out my last race. The Long Island Marathon is close, convenient and my annual hometown race, which I've done every year since 2000. My best in 2004 with a 3:31 and the 2008 attempt to qualify for Boston Marathon at 3:40 are some of my best times and within the first 7 miles of this day, my best effort will not get me close to that goal. There were massive amounts of fluids lost and absolutely no place to hide from the blistering heat. A 1:53 at the 13 mile mark and all this boy could do is hang on for dear life as I struggle to get from station to station and try to stay hydrated. Most of the day is a blur and the possibility of not getting home is on the table as I re-assess my goal times. Working to get in less than 4 hours and the blistering heat strikes me down with another couple of warnings as my legs cramp and my head goes into a spin.

I pull it back and continue to water myself down begging for the finish line. I am working hard and trying to salvage the day. I find some comfort in the fact that the entire field is walking up the Wantagh Parkway. I am not alone out there and misery is loving company! I manage to slug through the course and very unceremoniously cross the finish line in 4:15. On this day, I will take it, celebrate another finish and consider it a wakeup call for my ironman goals.

# Final Cycle

We are 12 weeks out until Race day and while the marathon serves as a long training day, the amount of hard-core training over the next 3 months will tell the final tale. It is a cycle that will continue with the last 3 out of 8 long distance runs of 19 miles, spread 3 weeks apart, an additional 8 of the 23 total 13 mile runs to be completed and 8 more 100 mile bike rides nearly encompassing every weekend in which 4 of those will be in the mountains! Toss in some routine 1 hour swims a few times a week, some additional park runs and various other types of miscellaneous training and you have yourself a recipe for success!

This little Betty Crocker, read it off the back of a box of brownies is nice on cardboard, but in order to execute this plan, we must be flexible, prepared to deal with adverse conditions and most of all patient. Plans change, things happen in life and one must be prepared to react and make adjustments. Despite the obvious nature of this advise, continuous reminders can be very helpful in finding the way. I recall procrastinating and finding excuses for not setting up my first Bear Mountain trip, as it is inherently a very difficult trip and the first one is always the most difficult. One thing however that I did not fail in doing is writing this one ride report and with that share the next section entitled Perkins Road.

## Perkins Road

The 100-mile century ride and the traditional follow-up 7-mile run has many names. Most commonly referred to as "Bear Mountain", but taken the form of "Bear II", "Yorktown Ride", "Yorktown Ride Revisited", "The Closer", but in this chapter, "Perkins Road," better understood for lessons later learned. No matter what the title given, it all comes down to the same thing, a long, hard, and at times brutal day in the saddle with a most difficult "cherry on top", that which is the 7 mile hilly central park run! Given the degree of difficulty of this ride and ensuing dishing out of pain, suffering and punishment, I tend to offer up my day to those less fortunate and in need of my prayers. I reflect back on my good friend, "Bernie the Attorney" whose wonderful wife Jen was diagnosed with cancer in her jaw and begins radiation treatment this week. I think about how, back in September, my dentist discovered an egg-sized whole in my mouth that rocked my world! I ponder the details of my diagnosis, the subsequent treatment, which included a 5-hour operation, including draining, shaving and using cryotherapy on the inflicted area. The result was nothing short of spectacular, a total and complete success! Having said that, my right lip is most likely going to be forever numb and at times quite painful. I found myself whining about that despite the fact that the outcome as a big picture item was so very fortunate. No cancer, no disfiguration, actual feeling in the lip (which I'm not sure is a good thing), but the alternative is "dead lip." I most certainly digress in getting to the details of the ride, and while the details are important for future learning, the set-up, approach and appropriate reflections are just as important. And while I keep Jen and Bernie in my thoughts on this day, I must refer back to a previous ride in which the death of a family, an aided suicide/murder by a spouse of his wife and two children buckled into the back seat of their vehicle. The vehicle parked atop of Bear Mountain and rolled down, instantly killing his wife! The children survived, but as mentioned in my earlier story, will have a tough road ahead. Besides the obvious reason for mentioning this story, the trip to Bear Mountain on this, the anniversary of that tragic event, but also the event on Friday that occurred during my 5th grade class that stirs up some major emotions and once again demands for a sympathetic, better understanding of the desperation, anger and confusion of some people that they would resort to ending one's life. The scene was horrific, as a young Korean man lies lifeless on the streets of Manhattan, just below the window from the gym in which I was teaching my 5th grade. The situation becomes desperate as the need to scramble to protect the children from witnessing such a desperate scene becomes the ultimate goal. The intensity of trying to successfully achieve this goal is magnified by the fact that just over a year ago to the date, this same group of children witnessed a suicide by a beloved junior in the high school. It was supposed to be just another friendly, spring day, in which the children played safely on the street, but on this day, nothing further from the truth was the case. Fortunately, the children were blessed in many ways. Leaving out the obvious potential disaster of more lives taken as a result, and emphasizing the heroism, quick action taken by the faculty and staff as the least amount of collateral damage was achieved. On a much smaller level, our school, but more specifically our department was once again faced with a situation in which quick response and an exit strategy needed to be provided and properly executed. We needed to somehow protect our children and try to shield them from these desperate, unexplained moments in life in which to the day nobody can seem to figure out why these things happen. My colleague's response following this situation says it best, "When I saw the fifth graders return happy and relaxed from PE, concerned only with catching the elevators, it was wonderful. I am so grateful to work with such an amazing team of educators. Thank you all and have good and peaceful weekend." And with that, I set off to Manhattan to tackle my first "monster" training session of the spring.

The marathon two weeks ago ranks right up there with 85 degree "temps" and nasty humidity, but the Bear cannot be matched. Certainly the gorgeous weather was a great way to start the day, but the list of uncertainties in navigation, physical ability and those "all too surreal" and unknown factors begin to creep in and draw the life out of me. It was only the second time taking this trip as a solo artist, but I tend to like it that way even though I love, "playing, playing in the band, daybreak, daybreak on the land." Despite all that is on my mind given the previous day's events, I begin to focus and take nothing for granted as I begin my rehearsal and mental imagery of all that I can recall to get to the George Washington Bridge. I carefully work my way to the Central Park, slide out on the North side and remember the path that takes me to Riverside Drive. I turn on Morningside instead as a familiar shortcut, but find myself lost! It's way too early to be lost and if that's not enough, I'm starring in the face of some steep hills to get my way back to Riverside drive. No big deal, unless of course you realize, that making a similar mistake around Perkins Road, will not be as forgiving as the streets of Manhattan. I re-focus, find my way to the bridge and attempt to navigate the hairpin uphill ramp that will never, ever, be a fond memory. The bridge is packed in both directions and rush hour in the city, on the bridge, is simply no fun! I finally escape the wrath of the "box car" trestles and hit some open roads. I settle in and begin to carefully pace myself and prepare to climb. I note each section of highway, taking a snapshot and filing it away for future reference. Many people are out on the course and so you're never alone. I remember thinking how wonderful it was that the roads were so nicely paved over, especially in narrow sections that seemed to be full of potholes. I flew through the section that leaves Nyack in my dust with no intention for a bagel stop which is all too often a tradition with group rides. I began to prepare for the narrow slopes and the brutal navigation through the dreaded Haberstraw and Stony Point sections. One section in particular is just an impossible pass that only got worse with construction. No chance for bikes and vehicles to share the road! Strap in and crank it through the half-mile section and hope the vehicle traffic is kind. It was an awful way to get it done and way too much in the way of chance. Plowing, searing and arriving at the "wall", is actually a good thing. Just before getting to the Park entrance and you know you have to tackle this serious uphill, followed by an extremely difficult descent. The wind is trying to take me out by grasping my 81mm rims and I will have none of it! Finally into the park and now begins a 10 mile uphill battle that takes close to an hour to the top. That's correct, 10mph becomes your average, tail between the legs speed, dropping below 5mph on some of the nastiest, steepest sections of the ride. And now the kicker! Hooray, I make it to the top and after just a moments rest and refueling, I begin the trip back down.

The road is bumpy, extra steep and unfamiliar. I start to think I made a wrong turn. My mind is just playing tricks on me, until I arrive at the bottom and there is no exit! Waaaaaaaaaaahhh!!!!!!!! I am visibly upset and slightly broken, but quickly shake it off and choke it up to some extra training. It takes me 20 minutes off my scheduled pace and concerns creep in regarding, not just an extra 20 minutes in the saddle, but the additional climb that was just added that equals the most difficult part of the day. Despite it all, it was time to head home and that is always uplifting and gives hope to a pretty rough day. The downhill is brutal, once again, strategically breaking and remembering how a vicious, mis-calculated downhill mistake will most certainly end your day. When I arrived at the bottom, the ambulance and 50 our more motorcyclists were on the scene. Sure enough, somebody dumped their motorcycle on the final hairpin turn and hopefully will make a full recovery. And yet, another solid reminder of the dangers of downhill's which didn't come to soon as the next section includes a climb out and a very open area with narrow shoulders to be executed to perfection and managed with extreme caution.

The drama slowly fades and the realization that the hills are less than a dozen to close this thing out! I get through Haberstraw and gear up for another couple wicked climbs including Rockland County, and the now very methodically calculated, less than a half dozen hills from Palisades Park.

The coolness of the day played a defining role in getting me home. Finally knocking on the George Washington Bridge and the confidence is building. Mentally, the work intensifies when you hit the city as traffic and pedestrians are out in full force on this beautiful sunny Sunday afternoon. Central Park greets me and my traditional victory lap is cut short based on my extracurricular mountain stage back on Perkins Road.

I'm feeling great and I lace up to close the deal on a run in Central Park. The mood is outstanding and although the population of people enjoying the day makes for a continuous, and difficult obstacle course. I'm loving it! The legs want to go for more and as I hit the half way mark, my time of less than 30 minutes is as good as any given day in the park. But then again, why not? Did you think you're playing with some kid in the park?

I chuckled and enjoyed a rare smile on the day as I polished off the museum mile and the last hill of the day. Back to the gym in an hour and the first of three "Perkins Road-trips" is in the books! My beautiful and loving family greets me at the door and we close the weekend with a barbeque by the pool and give thanks for all our blessings.

# Bird Song

I'm pretty certain that even the guards can't help to grin from ear to ear when Bobby and Jerry jam on that one at the Garden. My reflection on song and dance continues as it helps to move me and I begin to feel more at peace with the first Bear under my belt. I do realize that there is still quite the path to plow! It's alright, as I've been there before, I know the recipe and how to follow the instructions on the box and if I'm short one egg, it's all good and it will taste just as good. And so you look down the mouth of the beast and try to find some light at the end of the tunnel. The days and weeks and miles begin to fly by like the wind. I methodically follow my schedule and get stronger with each day. I battle through a blazing hot month of June, pushing off with yet another 13 mile run, 100 mile bike or rip off a 2000 meter swim which I'm now doing on a more consistent basis in my beautiful back yard pool installed last year! The ride to Montauk arrives and the flat, wind at my back 105 mile ride with a 7 mile brick run feels like a piece of cake compared to the hill fest in the mountains! It's yummy and fun and I have found a friend, that being the pain train! Peter Cotter and Thor are on the scene and we are loving life! We enjoy a gorgeous sunset at the Mantaukkitt, an evening sail and sweet accommodations by the club. The weekly training combined with various social engagements seems to become part of a lifestyle that is absolutely one of the major keys for making this dream a reality. The physical nature of the beast is being conquered with each passing week and suddenly I find myself peaking with improved finishing times on nearly every single training ride and run. I rip off a 2:32 on my last 19 miler and take a picture of my watch because I'm just not sure if it's all just a dream. Conditions were outstanding and I kept my eye on the ball, targeting each 6.5 mile loop at 50 minutes to stay on pace. It was the closer on 8 of those bad boys plus the additional marathon Sunday training run that sets me up and closes down the long distance run training!

My 7-mile park runs are coming in at under 8 minute mile pace with long standing records being shattered! I'm texting my colleague, Bobby Quinn and my wife nearly every other day with morning results and sharing with my Super Sports friends at camp.

I step back to consider the possibilities and throw serious caution at the wind. Intensity in training, if not monitored and carefully spaced can lead to injury. A lack of focus on any given ride can cause accidents. I begin to back off some of those sessions and carefully note the uncontrollable situations regarding traffic and accidents on the highway as they begin to rear their ugly, potentially race ending heads!

I have discussed in detail some of the tricky spots on my rides both locally and en route to Bear Mountain, but it's those unpredictable spots and situations that can catch you by surprise on any given day and wreak some monster havoc! It's those last couple of physical education classes or that last session of summer camp that someone gets hurt as exhaustion sets in and we lose or focus. Sure enough in my last two century rides in the mountains and on the local roads of Long Island, I manage to escape serious crash conditions within minutes of my position on the road. I would have loved to have embellished on a story about seeing a Bear and odds are with the amount of trips to the summit in future training years I just may, but as far as the car crashes go, my wish is to stay completely away from this drama pit! I just hit mile 92 across the George Washington bridge and as I enjoyed the view of the water to my right on Riverside Drive, the screeching of the brakes and crushing sound of medal was so close I had to brace for impact! It was less than 100 yards on the opposite side of the road, but already passed me when I looked back to witness a 5 car pileup! Breathing a sigh of relief, I continued on, a bit shaken, but extremely cautious. Hit the park for my 7 mile run and the heat forced me to walk to the various water stations in the park. All the warning signs were out and flashing on this last key work-out day and I had to continue to remind myself not only of last minute road hazards, but the dangers of going into the red zone on a 95 degree day!

I carried with me these thoughts as I took my final local century ride the following weekend, which would make 6 straight weeks of century riding! I was ripping it up and taking it home for yet one more final personal record!

Can lightening strike twice? You have to believe I'm thinking yes and my intensity increases in pursuit of that final trophy. I needed and addition 5 miles to reach the 100 mile mark and went off course for what amounted to 5-10 minutes. In that small span of time, I returned to Newbridge Road prepared to close out the day and came upon a car that was flipped on its side.

I was just minutes from being a serious part of this crash and in the span of 2 weeks, on my last century rides, I fortunately had a bit of luck and some wonderful levels of karma. I'm confident that my guardian angel was watching over me. The fire department was located directly across the street; volunteers emerged on the spot and safely rescued the trapped victims in the car.

I returned home safe and sound and knocked down another personal best with a 5:38 finish! The final hard-core week of training is complete! 6 centuries in 6 weeks, 240 bike miles on this week including an unprecedented 2 trips to bear Mountain, 8000 swim meters, 40 run miles and 2 personal training records! The 3,818 bike miles, 1006 run miles, 116,000 swim meters and some 96 strength training hours is complete! Stick a fork in me, I'm so done!

## Taper week

The most challenging part of my training appears to be complete, but taper weeks bring a brand new set of challenges. It's time to slow everything down. Back off the training gradually, check your equipment, fix things around the house and for goodness sake be careful! It's right around this time that I find myself on ladders, roof tops, up the chimney, down the stairs, playing with saws and all of sudden I have a new enemy. The Air conditioner leaks in the attic, which causes a flood and my daughters ceiling is destroyed. There is a bird somewhere in the walls of my house and the door bells wiring is threatening us with some sort of electrical fire from frazzled wires. The town refuses to give us a passing inspection on our fence for the pool, the hotel bills us more than a month in advance, and the walls are literally closing in around me! Is life always like this or is it customary to get kicked in the face when you're already down? Cynical, angry, desperate, out of control emotions take over and it's time to find some answers, solve the problems and not forget to breathe! It became quite comical and if we didn't laugh about these things and keep them in perspective, a crushing blow would be delivered and all the hard work to this point would have been wasted. I remember that as I tried to piece together and resolve some of these problems, tragedy struck on the roads of Long Island. I was particularly moved and visibly upset at the photo of the Father in the morning paper that spelled disaster! His 2 daughters ripped from him in this tragic car crash. The loss of his 19, and 20 year old daughters, as they traveled to camp in which they worked their summer jobs. I held Casey and Amy a lot closer that day and I'm a little ashamed at what I deemed to be problems in life. My prayers go out to those families that suffer such horrific losses and wish Godspeed on their recovery.

The week continues and I work diligently from my checklist, being especially careful, as the jobs around the home once again require some additional caution. I just don't recall that at any point during the year there was a need to be out on the roof, but there I was cleaning the gutters and fixing the drain that caused the damage to my daughters ceiling. There I was crawling around the attic that had to be 110 degrees as I attempted to locate and go to work on the damage, trying not to fall through the ceiling. There I was, carefully disconnecting and attempting to replace the doorbell. In one week's time, I'm suddenly a roof climber, attic dweller, carpenter and now an electrician? This can only happen during taper week because what would life be without more challenges? I actually don't mind all the diversions and consider them a blessing as my real fears of swimming in Mirror Lake with nearly 3,000 people in a mass start begins to crush my morale and drain my energy. I decide that diversion is the tactic that is working best for me and thus decide to call the race director and volunteer to play the National Anthem for opening ceremonies. I have been dreaming about and talking about doing this since 2004 and decided that this was the year to go for it! I'm so incredibly overwhelmed by the pressure in the swim that I must figure out a plan. Several emails to the director of promos ions and I decide to make the call to find out more details. I'm given the green light to do a telephone demo and with that put the telephone on speaker and blew my kitchen down! "Okay, James, that was terrific, when you arrive in Lake Placid, let's get together for a live demo and see how it goes." A brilliant strategy as I am now officially out of my mind scared of waking up on Ironman Sunday to face this day, but at least I'm no longer scared of the swim start, well, maybe just a bit!

## Mountain Bound

My favorite time arrives as the Jeep is packed and the 3 a.m. wake-up call is set for the mountains and I attempt to relive my childhood through my daughter's eyes while the city sleeps. A fantastic ride and upon arrival at 10 a.m. our hotel room is ready and this absolutely sets the tone for our trip and prepares us for race week. I go to registration and I am greeted by Mary, and Iron Lucha who are volunteering. The process is smooth and I am satisfied with 174 lbs. as my official race weight. I speak with the representatives at ASI, purchase my photo package and finally seal the deal on photos for my book. I do the traditional walk through the oval and unfortunately and as suspected the expo is limited in give-aways. I see a familiar face from N.Y.C. and it turns out to be Brian from Asphalt Green. Asphalt is the pool facility that we use for our swim teams as well as our summer swim portion of camp and Brian works with us on the scheduling of lanes. I'm excited, as it was a nice surprise to have Brian join the field. I continue on and have some peaceful, comforting words with one of the girls from the mission church. She invites me to attend their Baptist service as a tradition to pre- ironman race. I thank her for her gracious offer, but I have the "Iron Friar", 12-time finisher doing the mass at the local Roman Catholic Church, which can't be missed! I did express my concerns with the mass swim start of 3000 and the tricky downhill portion on the bike course and request prayers for a safe day, which was kindly, granted. I conclude my visit to the oval with some last minute purchases for back up spares, co2's, and treat myself to a hat. I test out the ironman performance drink being sampled and happily discover that the orange and red flavors will be served on the run course and the lime which I tried to use in training will be on the bike course. My plan was set and it will include having my own purple Gatorade in all my bottles out of transition and supplies at the special needs stations on the bike course. It's a little discouraging to have to supply my own, but fluids are up there with the most important part of my nutritional day and I must be able to consume the proper amounts to get to the marathon.

The day is slipping away and I head back to the hotel and review my list. At the top of the list is to contact the race director for the live interview and demo of the National Anthem. I eagerly make the call and was informed that the singer has decided to go solo and not use me as a backup. Despite my disappointment, there is a sudden calm in the room and a weight off my shoulders that allows me to focus on my race. Although my decision to add yet one more challenge to this day was brave and motivated by a long time dream, it was ripping the life out of me ,and destroying a race that I invested a lot of time and energy. I can make it happen one year, but perhaps a more thoughtful approach that involves some volunteer work for the race and allow the main focus to be on performing on stage with the harmonica in front of 10,000 people without staring down the mouth of an Ironman race would be more appropriate!

I immediately go down the list and check the items that need to be completed and the time line for each task. I fiddle with my race stickers, transition bags and begin to lay them out across the bed. I am thankful for the additional space in the suite we rented this year which allows me to keep my race gear separate from my regular luggage and all the families as well. The transition bags can be very confusing for first time racers and even in my 6th attempt at this race, items and special needs change and it's important to be meticulous with the contents of each bag. And yet, all this serious talk about bags begs my inclusion of a piece written years ago known as "Fullers ode to transition bags:" "When you sign in you will receive 13 bags: 1. dry clothes bag. this bag is to put your morning-of-the-race dry warn cozy clothing in after you change into your wetsuit at 4:30 am on the morning of the race. you will put this bag with all 1700 others in a big heap and Uber Volunteer Doug Fuller will sort them all out while you are racing. 2. T1 bag: put this on the T1 rack that has your number on it, a nice half awake lady will be there to help you. 3. T2 bag: place this on the other rack with your number on it. 4. Special Needs Bike Bag walk 1.3 miles up Mirror Lake drive in your wetsuit and bare feet and drop this on the side of the road near your number. 5. Special Needs Run Bag: place this on the other side of the road from bag number 3, no I mean 4. After you change into bag 1 you will swim then you will grab bag 2 and bike. Someone will take your wet suit and goggles and put them in the bag that was formerly bag 2, this bag now becomes bag 6. while biking you will grab bag 3 then you will stop biking and grab bag 4. Bag 4 gets emptied of its run contents and filled with your used bike stuff and now becomes bag 7. while running you will grab bag 5. after your done running you must go find bags 1,2,3,4and 5 (actually bags 2 and 4 became 6 and 7 so find those too) which are all in orderly piles which Uber Volunteer Doug Fuller organized into rows in ascending numerical order from left to right. If you can't find bag 2, it's because it's in the bag 6 pile (remember), if you can't find bag 1, look in the bag 5 area. bag 3 is typically misplaced in the bag 4 but bag 4 is now bag 7 so there is no bag 4 area....." and on and on and on and on........

The inclusion of this piece provides a small view into the mindset of the athletes prior to race day. Everything is being organized, yet nothing seems to make any sense. You question every move made to this point, check and re-check your lists, and try to breathe in an attempt to keep that fierce level of energy from unleashing too soon! I remind myself of the very long road that I have traveled to get to this point, review the few remaining details on my list, and that provides me with some levels of calmness. I check my schedule, "Swim one loop of the lake, enjoy a quiet dinner with the family, and meet some friends at the beach for our annual IBSEX." Yes, my little piece of paper lists all those things with actual time line. Seems simple enough? However, the solo swim around the lake last time ended in a panic attack and a race to the shore. No problem, I'll simply have my family take out a boat and shadow me. I am cautious, extremely respectful of the water and rules involving swimming, which dictates that you should never swim alone, are ruling the day! The plan is swiftly put into play and yet my wife and kids never quite get within 100 yards of me? I'm swimming the loop thinking, "What's the point?" I relax, swim a few more strokes and get into a zone. I simply leave it alone, push back the silly talk in my head, sing a few tunes from the 'Dead', and find my way home. "I'm a poet, I don't know it, my feet show it, cause I'm Johnny long-fellow." And with that, it's off to dinner and the beach. In short, dinner was nice, but the meet and greet at the beach was a bust! Mary and Iron Lucha, the only friends in attendance and the realization that this year's reunion of "blue page peeps" and "Garv- aid station hommies" will not be happening this year. The Mayor, Woody Freese, soon to be 12 time finisher of this race and in the company of only 4 others did not make our traditional toasting event. Woody is still the man and I enjoyed the little stat that he posted that includes his exceptional 100% attendance record at this event. I'm actually in the "every other year club" which distinguishes itself with 6 ironman finishes in the 12 year history and includes less than 50 participants over the years! However, things happen on race week that demands that the priority be on race preparation and so just a few proudly represented on the beach that evening. In honor of all my family and friends I close the night with my best rendition of "Little Red Rooster" and in keeping with tradition play a bitter sweet National Anthem to an audience of only 3, while looking out on Mirror Lake and accepting what will be.

The list on Saturday is short and to the point. I test ride the course, inspect the bike, drop bags and the bike at the oval, dinner, evening mass and to bed. Stay off your feet, stay out of the sun and hydrate! Use the wake-up call if available, set your alarm and for goodness sake, don't screw up the a.m./p.m button! Anyone keying in on this chapter to help race day preparation should note the simplicity and length of this paragraph as a critical reminder of what your pre-race day should consist of and let it be your greatest guide!

## Race Day

Race morning arrives in typical fashion, which includes awakening well before the alarm. Surprisingly enough, I slept well for a pre-race evening, but I am not feeling well rested. I'm a bit anxious and a tad uncertain of my morning management plan. I never want to be at the lake too early, but being tardy creates panic and that energy needs to be preserved. I follow my routine listed on my note pad and that helps to relieve some tension. My wife Karen is by my side with a comforting smile and words of encouragement, "You'll do great my Bear!" As always, Karen carries me for many miles and she will always be my greatest inspiration! I check in with my kids who are soundly sleeping, but I must depart with a hug and a kiss, which I manage without interrupting their dreams. I begin the trip down to the Lake to drop my transition bags and see John Lennon. No, I'm not hallucinating; it's a gentleman I met upon arrival to Lake Placid outside the hotel. We struck up a conversation and I told him that I was aware that he had done this race before because in my love for music, I can't help checking the participant list for the famous rock stars that will be joining me, and thousands of others on this day! We joked a bit more about the fact that Jim Morrison and

Brian Jones were not on the list this year as they have in the past and wished each other good luck. I made my way to the special needs bags area and it is a hike up that road, but happily unloaded the bags filled with Gatorades, extra sneakers, spares, Co2's and began my trip to the oval. Based on this year's plan I was definitely going against the traffic as the majority of people drop bags last, but based on my hotel and weight of my bags I needed to go directly to the spot. I can't help feeling like I'm in the scene in the movie "Midnight Express", involving a young Long Island man arrested for smuggling hash and tossed in a Turkish prison. He eventually finds himself in a psych ward in which the loony birds are all walking around a pillar and this guy decides to walk in the opposite direction against the grain! The feeling is quite disorienting and somewhat disturbing! I actually feel as if I have found myself in a land of very disturbed people (based on this event some might firmly agree) and to make matters worse I'm upsetting the conventional methods of pre-race preparation!

I come upon my friend Caryn; one of very few familiar faces and that helps to snap me out of it! I wish her the best of luck and continue to the oval to get body marked and make for final preparations. Everything is going according to plan and as I enter the bike arena, the gentleman is blaring on the loudspeaker, "3 minutes to get out of transition, you must leave now!" I removed the plastic covering, meticulously checked my bike, and worked my way to the exit. It is too warm to put on my wet suit, but I slip it on half way and begin the march up the hill with plenty of time to spare. I see an acquaintance that I met at the local pool and at this point just happy to see another familiar face. Mary and Iron Lucha are on the scene and would make up a big part of the limited personal fan base on the day. I see Bob Cook and his lovely wife just to the left of the chute and then I'm greeted by, Marc Roy, Jose Lopez and Rich Barkin at the swim start. The number of familiar faces continues to grow and at a time when it was most needed! I slide into the water waste high and then comfortably find a seat on the dock awaiting the start. I chat with a guy named Sam and share with him some advice on my swim plan to stay to the left of the line, as I have been successful in this approach in 5 previous races. Sam is appreciative of my advice, which is then magically confirmed by a public announcement: "Swimmers may swim to the left as long as you keep the far buoys to your left when reaching the outer points on the swim." I'm wishing that bit of advice I gave Sam was not publically displayed as I now fear 3,000 people going with that strategy and my little private Idaho becomes the scene of the "7" train in rush hour en route to Grand Central Station! I shake it off, push away the negative thoughts, only to have the new announcement hauntingly repeated over the loudspeaker: "My apologies, the race director has informed me that NO ATHLETES ARE PERMITTED ON THE LEFT OF THE LINE!" These are not the words I want to hear and have no intention of changing my strategy for this swim start! I begin to reflect on my many years of successfully completing the swim and don't allow any negative thoughts to enter into my train of thought. I notice that the time is drawing near as they prepare for the National Anthem and realize the stage is up at the pavilion and not on the pier as I imagined. I was thankful that the singer wanted to go solo and not use me as a back up as I think it would have cost many dividends and greatly affected my race.

In nothing short of that which is pure drama, the cannon explodes, the gasp from the athletes and the crowd and we are on our way! The crawl along the dock, the patient anticipation of the extreme numbers and massive amount of swimmers, and the plan is beginning to unfold. I find some space to the left and off I go!

Finally, the long awaited, incredibly stressful part of my day has begun and it's not so bad! There is so much anxiety that builds over days, weeks and even months that it's just an incredible feeling to no longer be worried and be able to unleash my energy. And still, I must be willing to get in with the pack! I begin to comfortably stroke and follow the path of bubbles in front of me that provides me with the only permissible form of drafting in the race. The questions begin to mount: "Will we be disqualified for being on the left?"

I push it away, smile and begin to sing. The tune from last evenings mass puts me at peace and I'm completely immersed in the swim, enjoying the coolness of the water and the indescribable calm which I'm experiencing. It is raining, but I don't feel a drop! I'm surrounded by nearly 3,000 other swimmers and I'm not getting touched! I was scared out of my mind at the start of the day and I no longer have any fear! Grace, and I don't mean the cute girl in the white cap swimming next to me, although that didn't hurt, but that of the Lord is with me!

I know the Iron Friar is in the lake as well and the prayers from the Baptist church continue to be my guide to safety. I emerge from the first loop in 42 minutes, right on pace and prepared to knock down the last loop. I settle in and pick up the pace and once again find myself untouched. The meters slide by, the turn around and then that grin that naturally makes up the lines of your face as you close down the last stretch.

The glowing lights from the Ironman swim finish neon lights and the roar of the crowd is slightly muffled from under the water, but become increasingly more vivid and surreal with each stroke.

I arrive at the beach at 1:21, and despite the long day ahead, I'm tickled to have reached this point. My family is, without fail, videotaping the scene, fist pumping through transition and thrilled to have arrived at the next section of the race.

## Bike Time

I cruise down to the oval, grab my bags and scurry to the tent. It's a mob scene so I wrap myself in a towel to maintain decency and slip into my bike gear. It's too warm for my vest and for the first time decide to leave the "rain-protecting, frigid cold, slide into Keene garment" behind on this tour. Out of transition in 11:30 and like clockwork in the mountains it begins to rain and then begins to pour! It is now "teaming" and I'm questioning my decision to bring the vest. To make matters worse, my speedometer is not functioning and I decide not to waste any more time after a lame attempt to repair the malfunctioning piece of equipment. "Is the rainstorm that continued for 13 straight hours in 2008 going to be today's fate?" Am I going to have to estimate my mileage and pacing all day and work this course without the use of my clock?"

The rain gradually tapers off, my speedometer becomes an insignificant piece of equipment and I'm happy to be climbing in the mountains. I realize that the ride to Keene is the time in which my speedometer is most needed to judge the speed and keep that section under control. I'm a pretty good judge of speed and rely on my instincts to get safely down the hill. The wind is at our backs, which is usually a good thing, but I'd prefer that scenario on the nasty uphill sections.

The day is flying by and the necessary task to begin taking on calories seems more challenging. I'm not hungry, but understand the value in replacing calories and having enough energy to continue to compete throughout the day. I'm scrapping down the bananas to raise potassium levels and avoid the "cramp monster!" I come upon the new section that replaced the traditional trip down and back on Hazelton road. The ride to the Ausable forks is gorgeous and adds yet another beautiful feature to this already magnificent course scenery. The ride into Wilmington is quite challenging and the mountain feels steep! The final stretch to Lake Placid, which is also up hill, is into the wind and throwing down yet another set of high hurdles!

I manage to get back to town, and as I swing by the special needs station, the volunteer graciously offers to hand me the contents of the bag. My strategy is to grab and go, get away from the transition area and have a quick visit with my family just around the corner. I arrive at our designated spot and a woman is warning us of the potential disqualification based on my families support. I know she meant well, but was making a scene and destroyed the short visit and reloading of supplies that we have enjoyed in previous years. Instead, it became a desperate attempt to get my drinks, food, and greetings in record-breaking time without drawing the attention of an official, which was hindered by the loud, whaling woman! I began giving orders: " Give me my drinks, come on I need my food, no, I don't want any spares!"

And as I climbed up the hill, the guilt of not being appreciative of my families continued support made for a tough trip through town. I felt bad, but knew they would understand my lack of patience and tolerance under the circumstances. I rode out of town with a 3:15:56 first loop split and was right on pace! The final loop requires an additional push as the conditions have improved with some cloud coverage on a humid day and roads are now completely dry.

The goal is to get in at 6:30 and negative split the course. I want to make up time on the hill and as I begin to max out with the wind at my back, I feel by bike sliding out from underneath me and the wind rips into my 81mm rims and tries to take me out! I refuse to lose and once again look at the big picture not allowing a few precious minutes gained on a downhill ruin my race.

I get down into the valley, tuck my head down into aero position, grind it out and continue to eat! Arrived at the Ausable forks down and out and take full advantage of this fast, flat section! All was going well as I attempted to open my last granola bar wrapper and found myself in a ridge in the road. I was trapped and about to get taken out! I re-established my hands firmly on the bars, ripped the pedals with everything I had and dug myself out! This was a nice little reminder to watch the road conditions as I approached the final portion of the course. It would be approximately 22 more miles, mostly uphill, the wind in our faces, which is even stronger then the first loop. I'm carefully eyeing my watch and attempting to calculate my closing time. I'm working hard and shoot for 3 p.m. to be out on the run course and have a shot at a personal best. Despite the difficulty level on the mountain, I feel energized and continue to push.

I bang the last hill and sprint into town trying to reach my mark. I'm once again greeted my Karen, Casey and Amy, relieved that they are not holding a grudge from previous transition. Instead, they are really excited and I know that I've put up some good numbers on the bike. A 6:30:56, 17.2 mph average and a negative split on 2nd loop of 56 seconds! Outstanding effort and I'm thrilled to lace up and get to the run course.

# The Run

Transition is 6 minutes and I fly out of town and down the hill. The legs are beginning to find the road, the heart rate is smoothing out and I have a shot at the title! I make the left turn and begin the long truck down the road. Suddenly, my right quadriceps renders me completely lame and forces me to the side of the road. I am only 3 miles into the marathon and I can't relieve the cramping. I attempt to stretch and I'm getting tighter with every movement. A volunteer offers to get me medical treatment and I adamantly refuse as to be in total denial that this is even happening! I drink my performance drink, pop some endurolytes and begin to walk in attempt to relieve the pain. "How can this be happening?" Is my race day over, my personal best out the window?"

I began to re-access my race. I had eaten like a champ, methodically taking in calories, fluids and supplementing with portions of banana at every station. I came to the realization that I had been traveling quite close to the "red zone" for the many remaining up hill, into the wind miles on the bike course. I ran out of town like a kid in a candy store and was paying for my over indulgence of sweet, delicious, marathon mountain roads. I chuckled a bit and found comfort in the fact that my legs were loosening up and I was back on the move. I was careful to keep the pace down in an effort to avoid being road kill on the course. I arrived at the end of the road, crossed the timing mat and realized I have one touch of this mat remaining and I am home free! In an attempt to avoid getting too far ahead of myself, I refocused and continued to plow up the road. The task of getting back to town on the first loop may be the most difficult portion of the run, especially given my recent blow-up at mile 3 and my refusal to walk. Steady, and ever so careful, but moving forward.

I manage the steep slope and the crowds are nothing short of spectacular. I felt like I was running through a stadium that packed the house like never before in this race. "Go James, you can do it, you're looking great!" just to name a few of the energetic, encouraging and continuous onslaught of remarks from a charged crowd. I spot the Armata's and they are screaming at the top of their lungs in excitement because I am now cruising and looking unstoppable! Wanda is atop the hill on my right, Mary and Iron Lucha on my left and the Runners edge guys including Cook and company just up the road. The lake run feels like an eternity, but the return trip as I pass my friends one last time before heading back out goes by quick. The mood is outstanding and the words "Final loop" is most comforting. I continue to plow past the field, moving up more than 300 spots overall and 18 spots in my age group on the bike; I have no intention of giving up any positions. The run is my back yard, central park is my oyster and the thoughts of one more training run begins to light fire under my, well, ya know!

I'm doing my best to stay in control and wherever possible offer assistance to my fellow competitors. I'm more than stocked with endurolytes, an electrolyte replacement capsule, and happily supply a woman requesting some at the aid station and another couple of guys down on the ground with severe cramping. I see Brian from Asphalt Green and he is working hard on the course. I catch my buddy Steve Tarpinnian from Total Team Training of whose "colors" I proudly wear and as a matter of good luck continue to suit up with in every big race for some additional good luck. I tell him to get ready to rack it up at Wise Guys, the local town bar in which we have created a post ironman tradition. He says, "I thought you weren't going this year?" I responded by telling him "Things change when everything is going well."

At this point it was all gravy as I had arrived at that final 7 mile run in the park that I did on a daily basis and makes this closer so much easier in my mind! I realize that my incident at mile 3 forced me to re-negotiate my goals, drop the pace and get home safe. I was fine with that and the day was almost done.

It was time to take it back into Lake Placid and as the flags that fly from the Olympic arena soar high in the sky and come into view, I begin to taste victory. I'm trying not to be over zealous and I have my mind directly fixed on that red zone meter. Do not blow up; continue taking fluids, yet at the same time, I need to get in under 13 this year.

I attack the town and do the math. I'm close and riding a thin line between cramping up and getting in! The excitement in the town once again moves me closer and as I carefully pace down the Lake in the final mile I grab a quick refill to ensure a safe landing. The final turn is made and I turn it up a notch and pass a few more people. The oval is in sight and I am going to get in less than 13 hours. The day is done as I climb an additional 54 spots overall and 15 spots in my age group and finish in a time of 12:56:36!

## Happy Hour

The day is done and it's time to celebrate with family and friends! The congratulatory messages begin to pour in over the phone and on the Internet. It was instant rock star status, at least for a little while!

I've never seen Amy and Casey so proud of their father then I have on this day and being the best role model I can be may be the biggest reward. Although the town was missing many key players that could not make the trip and those that were there racing made an early exit, good times emerged with some new faces and special friends.

Barbara Cronnin-Stagnari took the stage as the 5th place ironwomen finisher in her age group and made Mike Reilly announce her stellar 57- minute swim! Barbara hooked me up with great swim advice and introduced me to the course at Old Westbury, which afforded me some excellent closing rides, away from traffic and into the zone.

We raised our glasses as the sunset in the middle of town and the plans for next year's reunion ensued. Ken Jones, Christine Hill, Bob Spina, and Anne Vargas Halaby were just a few of the familiar names put to faces on this glorious afternoon. The family continues to grow and perhaps it's the great reunion in the mountains that helps motivate us to continue to push our limits and call ourselves ironmen and ironwomen!

## Life on the River

There remains to be one final challenge in the Adirondacks and that will include returning to the river for a class III-IV white water rafting trip. I battled with my girls and tried to convince them to go fishing, but like most cases I caved and provide them with an exciting finish to our mountain vacation. We travel 90 minutes to North Creek and despite our newly found experience from the last trip 2 years ago, I am still quite anxious about being on the river following the Ironman.

I do my usual solicitation with the top rafter, convincing him that we will need the top guide on the river based on the basket case of a dad that he is dealing with for this slippery slope of a trip. I get Todd to be our captain, which we called "The Todd". Many a high fives ensued as the man with 12 years on the river puts me instantly at ease.

The conditions are spectacular and my confidence is growing. The previous trip did not give Amy, my youngest daughter, the opportunity to row, sit up in the boat and enjoy a true Viking type expedition, but on this occasion, she proudly took her position. It was directly in front of me and it would not be long before I am snagging her on the shoulder and preventing her from being ejected into the roaring rapids.

We dice and slice down the river and it appears like we are in the clear with only one remaining rapid to go. Suddenly, the warning calls go out, a boat has capsized and the entire crew just up the river is dumped! Emergency procedures are signaled and it was amazing to watch all the rafting companies come together and work as if they were all one outfit. Each company, looking out for one another, and going into rescue mode. We pull a couple people in our boat, but the look on those rescued tells the story of fright and uncertainty as they patiently await the word on loved ones and other subsequent rescue attempts. Although it was only a matter of minutes before all passengers were accounted for, you can see the toll and affect it had on those most directly involved. A wonderful outcome, which included great team work, communication, and focus by all those on the river that day! A fantastic finish to a fabulous "Ironman: Journey To Lake Placid."...and God willing many more...

# Lyric Reprint Permissions/Acknowledgements

Music has been inspirational and nostalgically pleasing, a way to re-connect with so many special moments! A few lyrics or in some cases simply the title of a song were cited throughout the book that were representative of a particular moment and helped to capture those feelings and emotions. It is with great enthusiasm that I joyfully thank and acknowledge the many musicians and artists for providing such a driving force and tools for success!

Lyrics to Grateful Dead songs, " Looks Like Rain", "Eyes Of the World", and "Playing in the Band" copyright Ice Nine Publishing Company. Used with permission, gratis!

Lyrics to John Armata songs, "Always There" and "In the City" copyright John Armata Used with permission, gratis!

Lyrics to the "WASP" Words and Music by The Doors Copyright © 1971 Doors Music Co.,"Big River" Words and Music by John R. Cash© 1958 (Renewed 1986) HOUSE OF CASH, INC.(BMI)/Administered by BUG MUSIC,"Down By The River"Words and Music by Neil Young Copyright © 1969 by Broken Arrow Music Corporation, "Stumblin' In" Words and Music by Nicholas Barry Chinn and Michael Donald Chapman Copyright © 1979 by Universal Music - MGB Songs, "The Soft Parade" Words and Music by Jim Morrison Copyright © 1969 Doors Music Co., "It Ain't Easy"Words and Music by Ronny Davies Copyright © 1969 IRVING MUSIC, INC., "Runnin' Blues" Words and Music by Robbie Krieger Copyright © 1969 Doors Music Co., "Carry On" Words and Music by Stephen Stills

"Two of Us"

Titles of songs and other lyrics to be acknowledged including Queen's "Bohemian Rhapsody", "We are the Champions", and "I'm in Love with My Car", Black Sabbath's "Ironman", Francis Scott Key's "Star Spangled Banner", Baha Men's "Who Let the Dogs Out," The Who's "Magic Bus", Carly Simon's "Two Hot Girls on a Hot Summer Night", Giorgio Morader's "Let It Ride", Johnny Nash's "I Can See Clearly Now" Paul Simon's "The Boy in the Bubble", Bill Withers' "Aint No Sunshine", Eric Clapton's "Let It Rain", and "After Midnight" Billy Joel's "New York State of Mind", Frank Sinatra's "Making Whoopee", Gary Portnoy's "Cheers Theme Song", Rolling Stones' "The Last Time", Grateful Dead's "Little Red Rooster", Suzanne Toolan's "I am the Bread Of Life", Living Colour's "Cult of Personality", Led Zeppelin's "Your Time Is Gonna' Come, and "Rain Song", Eagles' "Peaceful Easy Feeling", and Jim Morrison's "American Prayer"

## A Note on the Author

James Armata was born and raised in Long Island, New York where he currently resides with his wife Karen of 20 years, and his daughters Casey and Amy. James graduated St. Anthony's H.S. in Smithtown in 1981, earned a B.S. at Brockport, his M.A. at Columbia at Teachers College in Physical Education and has been teaching and coaching at the Dalton School in Manhattan for over two decades. James has completed more than 15 marathons, dabbled in the "ultra" running world completing the Knickerboocker 60k and finished 6 ironman races at Lake Placid, which is the culminating point in each section of the book. He has written a sequel entitled Ironman U.S. Championship Bring It On Home detailing his adventures with the one and done Ironman in N.Y.C.

Made in the USA
Lexington, KY
02 September 2017